SENSE
AND
INCENSE

By Omar Eby

266

Herald Press, Scottdale, Pennsylvania 265

TO

Uncle Clayton and Aunt Martha Keener,

for all their kindness to me

that first year.

Acknowledgments

Small parts scattered throughout this book appeared during the past years in the *Youth's Christian Companion, Gospel Herald,* and the *Missionary Messenger.* Grateful acknowledgment is hereby made for permission to use those materials again. "Outcast Half-Caste" first appeared in *Christian Living,* April, 1964.

Appreciation also is expressed to Paul N. Kraybill, Paul M. Gingrich, Janet H. Kreider, and Anna Kathryn Eby (my good wife), for reading and criticizing the manuscript.

Again to Janet H. Kreider, and to Mary Elizabeth Lutz, a kind thank-you for "moonlighting" to prepare the manuscript.

Preface

Don't blame me—at least not entirely—for writing this book. In fact, I cannot even confess the pride or shame of having had the first idea to spin out "my Somalia story." Another one is responsible for that, but whom, I do not know.

This much I recall. It was a social occasion, and you know how it goes! Someone says a word; the conversation is picked up, added to, tossed on, and more words get folded in, carelessly, lightly, cheerfully. "Why don't you write about your Somalia experiences?" The words fell into place. A moment of silence, and then conversation flowed on.

Do blame me for this book for a few reasons. I hope to assist in destroying the cult glorifying the "foreign" missionary personality, by showing my very ordinary activities and routine living. I hope to appeal indirectly to the idealism of American Christians to give a few years of their lives in similar church services. I hope to show how God can take a common person with an ordinary background, use him in a program of the church, and through experiences, teach him a few facts about the Christian life.

Finally, I hope this little book will be a call to pray for the Christian witness, and for the national Christians in Somalia. In the past few years it seems as if stronger and stronger forces are contesting the right of the presence of Christian missions in a Muslim country, particularly of the small wedge the Spirit is driving into the Islamic Somali community.

O. Eby
Landisville, Pa.

Prologue

A blue-gray road runs south from Cearfoss to the first little knoll where it drops gently and curls among the farmlands.

The road awed me as a child. To wait for the rural mail carrier, as he came from Hagerstown (worlds away, to a little farm boy), I would cross to the other side of this road. I remember standing in the middle and pondering (as only a child might openly ponder at such simple truth) the fact that the road ran away from me in both directions and never met. And as I sat in the clump of tall grass leaning against the post that held the mailbox, I would thrill with ideas of the worlds, wide and lovely, lying at the ends of the roads.

When I think of those first seven farm years of my childhood, I somehow see a hazy violet or green, lazy with a round mellow yellow. The lawns spread out to the meadows, and the meadows rolled down to the stream. But my memories break through in fragments, hard to relate. The dull brick house trimmed in white and green . . . its cellar laden with pumpkins and green tomato pies, and rows and rows of pickles and applesauce in glass jars . . . the locust rail fence in the backyard . . . the cows, belching sweet clover breath . . . four ancient oaks, towering over the lawn, stretching black arms to the blind-eyed windows upstairs . . . and the road past the orchard . . . the road which led one mile to my first little world—the two-room country school in Cearfoss, Maryland.

When I was seven years old we left the farm for a white bungalow among a string of houses two miles north of Hagerstown. I remember the fruit trees—six apple, one cherry, and one pear—which walked over the hill behind the house.

Life consisted of seven reckless twelve-to-fifteen-year-old fellows who were content with the offerings of small-town living. But Father began to feel a mite uneasy about the influence of this easy summer-play on his youngest son. So he talked my married sister (who was living on a small farm with her farmer-husband, a herd of cows, and a few dumb chickens) into taking me for the summer months to do chores. There I was to learn something about a sense of industry, the processes of life, and the value of money. Instead, I simply learned to hate farm life.

My family being staunch Mennonites in their religious beliefs and living in a solid Mennonite community, I came under the influence of strong evangelical preaching. Sometime during my early high school days I had some small stirrings of uneasiness in my mind and heart about God and my relationship with Him. Eventually I made a public confession of my sins and acknowledged Jesus Christ as Sovereign of my life. This simple religious acceptance was to lead to a greater involvement.

I attended the Lancaster Mennonite High School in Lancaster, Pennsylvania, for my junior and senior years. Summers always took me back home to Hagerstown. But now these were spent in orchards, supermarkets, and on delivery routes.

While in high school I selected all commercial subjects. I felt that this would probably be the extent of my education, so I sought out the most practical subjects I could possibly find. But the summer after graduation, with big-brother counsel and my many feeble arguments, Father did a complete turn. I was allowed to go to college.

I chose to attend Eastern Mennonite College in Harrisonburg, Virginia. This little college, nestled among the

7

small hills in the beautiful Shenandoah Valley, fills me with warm feelings every time I return to it by memory or by car.

Upon graduation, I accepted a teaching assignment under the Eastern Mennonite Board of Missions and Charities, Salunga, Pennsylvania. I was sent to Mogadiscio, Somalia, East Africa. When my three-year assignment terminated in June, 1960, I returned to the States.

How shall I describe my sojourn in Somalia? Year after year of golden days piled one on the other. The country, the city, the ocean, the mission, the students—all this, and I don't quite know how to tell it. Yet, in this little book, I want to try to write about the golden glories of my newfound homeland, and her people.

Contents

List of Illustrations

Chapter One

Mogadiscio (i)

New York . . . *The Liberte* . . . French . . . *"Oui, Oui, Monsieur"* . . . pickled mackerels . . . beetroot salad . . . sky, water, water, sky . . . position, Lat. 45° 53′ N., 39° 02′ W . . . Paris . . . Eiffel Tower . . . Notre Dame . . . sidewalk cafe . . . bloody, tough steaks (fought like a barbarian to eat them) . . . trains across Europe . . . Karlsruhe . . . Sixth Mennonite World Conference . . . college friends now turned Pax men . . . more trains . . . Switzerland . . . plunging water . . . glass lakes . . . snow glistening purple and pink . . . always the green, green hills . . . Italy . . . Rome . . . Vatican . . . Michaelangelo . . . Byzantine Period . . . colossal Colosseum . . . Trevi Fountain ("Three Coins in the Fountain") . . . spaghetti . . . vegetable salads nutritiously, deliciously pampered in oil . . . the Catacombs . . . skulls, bones, mummies . . . figure of the fish . . . night flight from Rome . . . Khartoum . . . Africa . . . horrible, hot Aden . . . "home" to Mogadiscio.

And that was my twenty-two-day trip to Somalia in two hundred words.

I shall never forget that night flight from Rome over the Mediterranean. Dawn pinked as the whispering giant "Alitalia" plane screamed to a halt at Khartoum.

It was five-thirty in the morning. We transit folk found tables in the airport restaurant at which to eat breakfast. Here I met for the first time two characteristics which I was to meet in every African restaurant I ever ate in: table linens which were damp to the touch and waiters costumed in long white gowns and red fezzes.

The tables were partially set. Glasses and cups were turned over. Clean serviettes covered the utensils. Nearby at another table, one sleepy Arab waiter was shuffling about, turning the glasses and cups into their positions, and filling cups with coffee.

Eager for a drink of stiff coffee, I turned over my cup. A cockroach ran from under the cup, crossed my plate, and was on to the table where it hid under the next plate. I gasped and quickly glanced to see if anyone had noticed. The other folks were absorbed in newspapers, or sitting with their heads propped in their hands dozing.

That was my first introduction to Africa—and I rather liked it.

Half a day later I saw my city, Mogadiscio, clinging to the coast, and half an hour later I met my new "uncle" and "aunt," Clayton and Martha Keener.

I did not unpack that night; we all climbed into the Chevy "Suburban" and headed for a place in the bush called Mahaddei. There I saw my first "unzooed" camel. In fact, I saw a herd of four hundred of those stupid beasts. I wouldn't walk a mile for a camel now!

But I was not a bushman; I was in the city with twenty-four-hour electricity and "yellphone," Somalia's version of a telephone.

The mission in Mogadiscio was housed in rented quarters, a two-floor, four-apartment, white stucco building. The Keeners and I occupied the two apartments downstairs. Upstairs, the mission had rented one apartment for classrooms, which comprised our English night school. An Italian family resided in the other upstairs apartment.

From the flat roof, the Indian Ocean, a few hundred yards away, glittered in the sunlight. Blocking the view of ocean activity from the ground floor, the largest Somali hospital in the country lay across the street. It consisted of many low one-floor buildings, covered the equivalent of several blocks, and was completely enclosed by a high wall, except the side facing the ocean.

Next door to us was the Supreme Court, a small, unimpressive building of peeling plaster and one lone guard. On the other side was a three-story apartment. Italians lived below; on the second floor two Arab brothers lived with their several wives and babies. On the third level, a small herd of children played.

As was common for most properties a few streets away from the business section of the city, a stone wall surrounded the building which housed the mission headquarters. Two huge red iron gates closed out the street activity, and thus created a small courtyard. A few small trees and bushes grew reluctantly in the corners.

I usually rose at six o'clock to put in an hour of work or reading before breakfast. The first months I spent some time attempting to learn the Somali language on my own, with occasional aid from a Somali informant. Those hours at language study were always in the morning from eight to ten-thirty.

There were several reasons why I did not learn the language. There was no class, and no teacher. I was not given time to study it but rather, was assigned to my teaching job the third day on the field. Somali is an unwritten language. Italian was the official language; Arabic the religious language. Then, too, I had not yet learned to enjoy working with foreign languages. Finally, one could move about the city using English and Italian.

This long list of reasons for having not learned the language is not so much an alibi as it is to show why I admire my mission colleagues who have acquired the language. But then, I have at least been spared one of the sins so peculiar to missionaries: pride in handling the nationals' language!

At ten-thirty everyone dropped his work and circled the table for tea. For fifteen minutes we swapped news, brought each other up-to-date on what we were doing, and planned those activities which involved us all.

The flavor of Somali tea borders on poetry! It may be a bit difficult to describe in a narrative account. Tea is used, of course, and water. Also sugar, cinnamon bark, a pinch of salt; cardamom seed, which in the Somali language is called "hell," gives it a distinct thick spicy flavor. I was immediately addicted to the tea! Some botanist should check cardamom seed for a habit-forming drug! Or something it was that makes Somali tea so irresistible.

Everything downtown closed at one o'clock and stayed shut until four. We took a "siesta" from two to three. At four, when the school opened, the city was also stirring back to life. Classes in our English night school ran from four o'clock to nine, with an hour off for supper. After school closed in the evening, there were always lessons to prepare, homework to correct, a game of Scrabble or chess, reading, letter-writing, and the town to stroll through.

It was such a common occurrence—now that I think of it. I hardly know why the memory of it all stirs me. It is a memory of those frequent night walks through the city.

It was nine o'clock or ten. Night classes had ended. A few students lingered by my desk to ask or say. Then we would step out into the night, bright with a low moon lately risen from the cold ocean-black.

And then some student would say, "Will you come drink tea with us, Mr. Eby?"

And then I would say, "But you have been so kind and I have drunk of your tea so often. Will you come drink something cool with me in my house?"

"No, you come with us, Mr. Eby. We will find some clean teashop where we can sit and talk."

"And what shall we talk of as we sit?"

"We shall talk of English and Americans, Somalia and independence. . . ."

". . . And friendship and God?" I would ask.

"And friendship and God," some student would echo.

Then I would think a little prayer to God for a chance to say something about Jesus. And probably some student was thinking to say something about Muhammad.

So we sat and drank tea and talked. The kind hush and sweet coolness of the city night caused us to open our hearts. We talked—sometimes as teacher with students, sometimes as friends, more often as brothers.

In the late evening I would sometimes wish that Jesus were walking the dusty streets again. I wanted my students to see Jesus and meet Him. Then I would remember that they were to see Jesus in me. And I was humbled.

The Keeners and I had a kind of communistic living arrangement. We kept a tin can "kitty" in the safe. Each of us contributed equally. That meant that we all had access to it, too. I could go out and buy anything I was hungry to eat. They did the same. When it was very much in price, we usually consulted the other "kitty-holders." This fund paid our food, electricity, water, the garbage collector, and our one houseboy.

The living quarters were simple, but comfortable. Our few modern conveniences sometimes proved to be cantankerous: a washing machine which threatened to electrocute its operator, a bathtub that leaked, and locks which wouldn't unlock.

The little rusty key turned once. I turned it again, three times, a dozen. Nothing happened. I tried again. Kneeling at the dull old latch, I looked at it imploringly. One keyhole eye stared back blankly from under the long-eared handle.

"Can someone help me?" I asked and tapped on the door.

When no one responded, I tried the hocus-pocus flip-flip of the key again. It turned over and over—a dozen times, two dozen, three. Now don't panic, I told myself. You're only locked in the bathroom.

It was my first week at the city mission home and I was trying desperately to appear as if I were normally adjusting to the routine of mission life (to which I had been oriented while in the Occident). And now this. No one had told me in the manuals for new missionaries how to cope with latches and locks on WC doors. But I could see it now—that chapter heading in the manual I'd write! "How to Lurch the Lock on the Latch of the Lavatory Door."

The second time I rapped I got an immediate response.

"Stranded?" a smiling voice quizzed from the other side.

"Yes, ah . . . I guess I should have studied engineering."

"Now lift up on the door with the handle and apply pressure by pulling toward the left. Begin turning the key in the direction as if you were locking it. Then when you've turned it about halfway, turn the key quickly backward twice—to the right, I believe. But keep bearing down on the key while you do this. It should open; it always works for me." I thought I detected just a shade of you-stupid-dope in Aunt Martha's voice.

I had begun to wonder if I might spend a considerable amount of my three-year term as missionary teacher in the confines of my toilet. I couldn't climb through the window. This was the city; the mission had taken the only sane precaution of putting bars on all the ground-floor windows. I had never seen a house in that city that had first-floor windows without bars. But I soon learned to cope with Italian locks as well as with most of their other bits of baroque equipment.

The Keeners traveled to Nairobi, Kenya, for their month's holiday. With them in another car, the Roy Shirk family and the Victor Dorsch family left for vacation, too. I was alone (of Mennonite mission folks) in the city, and my three Pax buddies, Chester Kurtz, Allen Brubaker, and Marvin Musser, were alone at Torda, 280 miles south of me.

Both they and I tried to figure out a way in which we could get together for a bit of fellowship. I had never met them in Somalia. Only Chester I had known earlier in the States. We were too poor to travel the three hundred miles at our own expense. Neither could one charge it against mission travel without a good reason. Five weeks wore away and we never did get together.

Soon afterward, the three Pax fellows did come north to Mogadiscio. With them were Curvin Buchen and Nevin Kraybill, Pax fellows visiting from Tanganyika. "Now we are six," we said with Winnie-the-Pooh.

We were together for a week. In that week the six of us sang and sang and sang. We sang in the mornings and in the evenings, at our worship services for the Somalis, and at the vesper service for Europeans, and again at the regular prayer fellowship on Sunday evenings when the Sudan Interior missionaries and we Mennonites met conjointly.

Although it was the first that I had met the fellows, it was a good meeting. The first several days were rather uneventful, but by the third day they began to emerge as individuals. By the end of the week we were acting like old buddies who might have known each other for years.

That was just part of the foreign living—a demand for rapid adjustment regardless of the situation. It was so seldom that we Somali missionaries saw other Christians that when we did meet with some, we would accept them with open arms. This was much different than at college, or in our tight little Mennonite communities where we could select who in our minds (correct or not) were the good people we wanted to know and love. This was a good lesson—this demanding acceptance of everyone who moved through our mission home.

They said that it was to be the cruel world. But I did not find Mogadiscio cruel. Oh, there were the continual stares I got for being an American with pink toes and straight hair. But that was not exactly cruel. It was more like being indiscreetly curious. Perhaps what cut me the most was their idea that if we were Americans, we must be rich and stupid. That was rather cruel to my ego, I must admit.

For some time the mission had been searching for a suitable property to buy in Mogadiscio. They found such, one month. An old Italian ex-big-game hunter wanted to sell a property on which he was living. It was about forty years old. For the past several years the buildings and houses had not been kept up with repairings and paintings. Now suddenly, with the purchase of this property, all my mornings were spent at painting and tearing out cactus bushes.

Chapter Two

Aunt Martha

"Welcome home!" my hostess said.

I stepped into the cool living room of the mission house.

"And make yourself at home," she continued. "We'll just tell you as we do all our guests and the people who live with us—make yourself at home. If you need anything and don't see it, ask for it. If we have it we'll get it. If we don't have it, we'll show you how to do without it!"

That was my introduction to a little gray-haired lady warmly known among the Somalia Mennonite Mission staff as "Aunt" Martha. That was also my introduction to Aunt Martha's homespun philosophy which wove through her life like a golden thread, hallowing and brightening the work of all who lived with her.

"Want a drink of limewater?" She held out the glass. "Ever see an ostrich egg? We eat 'em here." She turned the monstrous oval slowly in her hand. Seeing the look of disbelief on my face, she laughed. "Oh, but it is not barbaric to eat them! Good scrambled or in angel food."

Aunt Martha came with her husband, Clayton, to Mogadiscio, Somalia, in August, 1957. They lived there for one year. He served as the acting director, while the former director and his family were on furlough. Aunt Martha joined me in teaching English in our night school.

The Keeners had spent the past seven years next door to Somalia with the Ethiopia Mennonite Mission. Although grandparents, they kept pace with the youngest of the mission family. Known as "Mamma" Keener to sixty blind boys in a school sponsored by His Imperial Majesty, Haile Selassie, Aunt Martha conducted Braille classes and craft classes in weaving and knitting.

Aunt Martha can unpretentiously preface a story with, "One morning when Clayton and I were called in to face the king . . ." or "One day when His Majesty was visiting the School for the Blind. . . ." But now they were on a one-year loan to Somalia, their eighth year in East Africa.

While our Muslim students prayed on Friday, we took to the beach to swim, tan, hunt shells, or, as Aunt Martha used to say, "to see what the sea had thrown up!" Dripping and burning from sun, sand, and salt, we drove back to our apartment, eager for showers and hair-washings. Aunt Martha emerged from the bathroom drying a disheveled halo of hair, and headed for the kitchen where she began kneading biscuit dough.

"Wormy flour you brought the last time, Omar."

"Really," I answered, not at all surprised.

"The next time you go, I want you to take my flour tins along and weigh directly into that. I want that little old Arab man to get accustomed to the sight of you or me with those cans, so he'll know to give us good flour. And if he doesn't recognize you with my flour tins, tell him it's for the old woman you live with, who bakes and gets angry when you bring bad flour."

A cautious knock on the front door interrupted the kneading. Two lady doctors were calling for their regular Friday evening class in conversational English.

"Bless you! I forgot all about this class. But come right in; we'll go through with it!"

The Italian ladies made sweeping gestures of refusals and mangled a few apologies, saying something to the effect of waiting until next week.

"Not at all, not at all! Come in. Right now!" Aunt Martha insisted. Her voice was so warm and her manner so genuine that the Italian ladies soon forgot her appearance.

With her hanging, kinky hair tangled in a bright red bow, and kneading dough with one hand, Aunt Martha wrote English sentences on the chalkboard.

The Keeners and I had agreed early that year not to conduct any classes on Friday afternoon and evening. Sunday was so full with the various religious services that we declared Friday our day of rest.

Early Friday evening was usually the only time that it suited many of the Italians who wanted private tutoring in their English. Uncle Clayton and I had manipulated all our private students into hours during the week, stubbornly holding open Friday as our own.

Only Aunt Martha could never say "No" to a student, when there was standing room only in her classes; or to an Italian who paid well for private lessons, when it took another hour from her housework; or to a missionary colleague, when it meant another assignment, a speech, prayers, or a trip to the village. But then, only Aunt Martha was selfless.

"Two packages! One for us and one for Omar!" Uncle Clayton came to a stop in front of the mission door. He

22

hugged two rather badly torn boxes between his legs on the footrest of the Vespa motor scooter.

"Would you believe it!" glowed Aunt Martha. "Who would remember us?" She went immediately for a pair of scissors to undo the cord.

"What the earth!" exploded Uncle.

"Oh, it is wonderful! *Kool-Aid!* Wonderful, cool *Kool-Aid!* Packs and packs of it!"

"Hundreds and hundreds of them!" commented Uncle Clayton with just a catch of a grumble in his voice. "And nothing else!"

"But think of all the people we can give drinks," announced Aunt Martha, her optimism soaring.

"Now who would have thought to send that?" inquired Uncle.

"Well," Aunt Martha began slowly, "you see, in this letter I wrote to a Sunday-school class of grandmas, I just mentioned that we offer cold drinks to anyone who comes, because it is such a welcomed thing in this hot country, and so few Somalis have any refrigeration. And I just made a tiny hint that I did get tired of squeezing all those limes for lime drinks and that I sometimes wished for something quicker when an unexpected visitor dropped in. But, oh, isn't it wonderful how the ravens feed us!"

We, and the students, and all our guests settled down to a long routine of drinking *Kool-Aid* of every imaginable color, all having the same flavor. Aunt Martha became quite adept at mixing various packs for varying color schemes. Yet after the fiftieth pack of *Kool-Aid,* one could not possibly distinguish between flavors. It was all one with only colored variations of the same theme. I had learned to tote a single glass of *Kool-Aid* for hours, knowing if I ever emptied it beyond the half I would get an unwelcomed refill.

The next week a second box of *Kool-Aid* arrived from the States.

"Martha," Uncle Clayton whimpered, "is every member of that Sunday-school class going to send us a box of *Kool-Aid?*"

"How do I know, dearie? But just think of all the drinks we'll be able to serve. . . ." She caught a glimpse of Uncle Clayton's face.

"Martha, do you know that we now have enough *Kool-Aid* on hand to fill a 250-gallon tank?"

"But, dear, it is a gift."

"But we must buy sweet water and sugar. It'll take 200 pounds of sugar to sweeten that!"

Uncle Clayton was not angry; he was just the practical side of Aunt Martha, serving to pull the household routine and finances into a more sensible balance.

"We must pray more for those women in my morning classes," Aunt Martha announced at the dinner table one noon. "This morning Fatima came to class late all in tears. Of course, the other women and I wanted to know what had happened. Here, didn't her husband send their son away to a boys' boarding school in Hargeisa. He made arrangements, bought clothes and an airplane ticket—all behind her back. Just told her about it an hour before he came to collect the little fellow to take him to meet the airplane. I knew that she was divorced from her husband. She poured her whole life into that child. And now this. I think it's cruel. And he's only ten. She worked at the Somali hospital, and was studying some English on her days off, hoping to get a house job from some American oil people."

Aunt Martha's heart was tied closely to the women in her English classes. Her friendship for these Somali women always went beyond that of a teacher. Many times she came down midmorning to the apartment from school to get aspirins, Merthiolate, bandages, or alcohol. These she would tote back upstairs to clean cuts, to dress wounds, and to dispense for headaches.

"Fatima wailed that there can't be any God watching over her life if He allows such to happen," continued Aunt Martha. "I was so surprised to hear her say that. I thought all Muslims just instinctively threw up their arms at anything and cried, 'God wills it!'"

And so we prayed for Fatima and all the other women in Aunt Martha's classes, not only that noon but constantly throughout that year.

There was a tremendous bustle in the house one night. The Keeners were invited to the United Nations office for a party in honor of some dignitary visiting from the UNO offices of New York.

Aunt Martha was being her usual bit late in getting ready. In the last-minute scurry she snatched up her carefully folded black woolen stole and dashed for the car.

On the way through the main entrance of the UN headquarters to shake hands with the host and hostess in the receiving line, Aunt Martha shook out the stole and began to drape it about her shoulders. Suddenly she was struck with horror to see legs and straps drop from the folds.

The carefully folded black woolen stole which she had grabbed in haste turned out to be her old-fashioned black woolen swimming suit.

With one deft scoop she gathered the garment in her hands and passed it on to Uncle Clayton. "Would you mind returning this to the car," she said with a little laugh. "It's such a warm night. I was foolish to have brought it!"

Aunt Martha gave of herself constantly and of her possessions again and again. She was always surprised when students brought flowers, papaya, or bananas. She was even more surprised when the Italian lady students brought bottles of *vino italiano* at Christmas. That first Christmas she must have received a dozen *dolce* cakes, a light, spongelike cake dotted with rum-flavored raisins, a cake of great rank among Italians.

"They are all so kind," she would cry joyously and run off to give them a drink of *Kool-Aid* or scrape together some small item for a return gift.

The Italian wines we tried unsuccessfully to return to the givers. We attempted to explain to them that we do not drink and it would be indecorous for a mission to offer it to any of its guests. Usually by then the givers had lost their Christmas spirit.

"And the Somalis are commanded not to drink alcoholic beverages. Whatever will we do with it?" groaned Aunt Martha when the guests had gone.

"Transfer some of it to an old catsup bottle so Mohamed, the cook, won't know what it is, and use it in cooking," someone suggested.

"Five bottles! It would take five years to get rid of it, no more than I ever use in cooking," Aunt Martha said.

"Send it to Nurse Helen and let her use it in her clinic for cough syrup," another suggested.

"Perhaps we had just better empty it in the lavatory," offered Uncle Clayton.

Aunt Martha was a skilled cook. Yet she occasionally lacked confidence in her skill. Invariably we would hear her muttering to herself in the kitchen. "Oh, dear, I wonder what the ravens are going to feed us."

This was a favorite expression of hers. I dared to tamper with it one day when I stopped by the kitchen door and said, "I do not wonder *what* the ravens are going to feed us; I wonder *if* the ravens will feed us!"

"*If* they don't feed us, we'll eat *them!*" she retorted with a chuckle.

The first year had passed quickly. I was being transferred for five weeks to Mahaddei, our inland station, seventy miles north of Mogadiscio. When I would come back to Mogadiscio a new director would be in charge. The Keeners would have returned to Addis Ababa, Ethiopia.

It was a long seventy miles that I wended alone to Mahaddei. They were long because I had just said farewell to Uncle Clayton and Aunt Martha, who had opened their home and had taken me in as a son. The adjustments to overseas mission work and to a foreign culture were considerably lessened or were not at all. They had very wisely eased me into my work.

I drove on through the quiet night and arrived at the dark mission house at Mahaddei. The two-hour ride alone had given me considerable time for reflections. I went straight to the office and wrote the following letter to the Keeners.

"It's night and all the mountains of the morning have long quietly dissolved in the shadows of the late hours. They are still there—those mountains—but I view them as hills from this distance.

"Yes, it is night, and the psychologists have taught (and it seems a sound thought) that in the night the heart is more frank, and the words of confession more free and sincere, and the soul more pure in its love. Indeed, I find this to be true.

"One year has been the length of one short month and in it I find food and thought for future years. For when

27

I was rash, as only young ones can be rash, you were kind with the mellowness of age. When I sulked with the weary boredom of the task, you continued with the steady refreshing strength. And when I doubted some little promise, you showed me by life to a greater faith. And so I go on.

"At night one remembers all the little joys of the day, and he takes them out one by one and turns them over in his mind carefully. He does not ask why they are joy, for he knows that at the mere cold analysis they will flee. So it is at the night of this year; I remember all the pleas-antries . . . ice cream at eleven . . . learning chess . . . winning Scrabble . . . Somali tea, cookies, and pumpkin . . . united prayers . . . sea lunches . . . arguing subjunctive conditionals . . . challenging the pronunciation . . . wash-ing clothes . . . chatting over the dishpan. . . .

"It's night and one must sleep. Yet he fears, for the morning and the new year are different. They are not the same. This he knows and fears.

"But you have prepared me for the morning and the new year."

Chapter Three

Mahaddei

"Nabadt, Ma'alim!" The screen door slammed.

I looked up. One of the Somali teachers stood just inside the door.

"Se tahai?"

"It is peace."

"Ma faida?"

"I am well."

"Ma bariden?"

"Yes, we were safe through the night."

Hassan scowled down on me from his station at the door.

"You are not a very good student. Will you ever learn Somali?"

"Perhaps I do not have a very good teacher!"

Hassan, the oldest and least educated of the three Somali teachers at the Mahaddei boys' boarding school, not only took a dim view of my language ability, but frequently said so. Yet, this was perhaps the simplest of the problems we had in understanding each other.

29

I was sent to Mahaddei to keep the school open during the director's emergency leave. I lived alone, for there was no other person on the mission compound at Mahaddei, and for that matter, no Europeans lived in the village or nearby.

Perhaps this is why Hassan carried a voluminously inflated opinion of his importance on the school's staff. He was only the teacher for grades one and two, but had come into the idea that he was to be something of an acting director or principal in the absence of the headmaster. My being assigned to the school was smiled upon by Hassan with a kind of condescending pity. He programmed the school day's activities and even took it upon himself to speak officially for the mission. Yet all this was done coyly, not behind my back, but more as though he were attempting to save face for me, to protect my soft head from the students and the public.

"What ever will we do? It is too bad!" he might begin.

"About what?" I would ask, annoyed.

I was to agree that indeed it was terrible and that I had not the smallest notion of what could be done before I was told the day's current tragedy. I had been sent from Mogadiscio only a few days ago and still played the game rather poorly.

"Now what's wrong?" I asked pointedly.

"A boy ran away."

Great tragedy is eloquently uttered in simple language.

"Well, that makes one less to teach! Is he mine or yours?"

The silence, pregnant with gloom, deepened.

"Mr. Eby, this is very serious."

"Why?"

"He is only a small boy of twelve. He is from the city.

30

Perhaps he is trying to walk the whole way to Mogadiscio. Seventy miles!"

"Maybe he is hiding here in the village."

"No, someone has seen a boy walking to Johar."

"Well, if he gets to Mogadiscio, perhaps his father will beat him and bring him back."

"But what if he doesn't get to Mogadiscio? The hyenas, the heat, the bushmen!"

"He'll probably come back. We can't make them stay if they don't like this place. This isn't a government school."

"It will be a great shame on the school if we allow a boy to run away and we do not show any care. The village will talk."

"Okay, what do you want," I inquired, not from fear of village gossip, but to get to the bottom of his concern for this boy.

But Hassan was not finished playing his game. He never was.

"Let's go speak to some of the old men of the village," he offered.

"Perhaps they can tell us what to do."

The mission compound stood on the edge of the Mahaddei village. It was about a quarter-mile walk to the center of the village.

"Have you had breakfast, Mr. Eby?"

"No. I was going to have it, but you insisted that we come to the village."

"I am sorry. Let us take some tea here in a shop."

The teashop decor was typical: small rough-top tables, folding chairs which pitched one on an obtuse angle, a tightly packed dirt floor, and sober, thick glasses of khaki-colored tea. The spicy tea lifted my spirits, exactly what I believe Hassan had intended.

"I think we'll call on the mayor first," he said.

At this point I didn't offer any further protests. Yet the idea of involving the mayor in our student problems irritated me considerably.

The mayor was sitting outside the door of his house absorbing the early morning sunlight. He was hugging his one leg pulled tightly against his chest, rubbing his fingers between his toes, and yawning.

After shaking hands and inquiring if everyone had peace, we followed the mayor into his house. Business of this importance had to be conducted within the privacy of his house. A village has ears!

After what seemed like hours of discussing and arguing in Somali and in English, it was decided that someone should travel to Johar, the nearest town with a telephone, and call the father of the boy to discover if his son had arrived in Mogadiscio.

"Is this not the best thing to do, Mr. Eby?" Hassan asked.

"Hassan, you will have to go to Johar to telephone. I will take your classes. Hurry back as soon as you can." I tried to sound as if everything was under my control. Yet I knew that Hassan had maneuvered me to his point.

Hassan left for Johar on the morning's only bus and I turned back to an awaiting roomful of thirty-five first- and second-grade youngsters.

"What is this?"

"This is a booook!" They screeched back.

"What is this?"

"This is a peeennn!" They screeched again.

Little black parrots, I thought, screeching out white men's words. What did it value? Perhaps little now, but they were intent on learning the English language. Perhaps among the bobbing, twittering little parrots there

was another Nkrumah or Jomo Kenyatta in the making.
More likely they thought of themselves as future Nassers,
at least not Haile Selassies!

Dinner had to be bolted, for three leathery men had
arrived at the house requesting me to take them, the government clinic dresser, and a policeman in the mission
car to the bush.

"A woman has been found dead."

"They think somebody drowned her."

"We want to go and make an investigation."

"You will take us?"

"And the policeman?"

"And the clinic dresser?"

"We will pay you something."

They kept a constant stream of questions among themselves. Finally, when their mission was completed, they
sat back on their chairs, and eyed me for a decision.

"Will you all come back with me?" I asked.

"Yes, all of us." One smiled.

"Why do you ask?" Another quizzed.

"Oh, perhaps you just want a quick way to go to another
village. It is very hot now and the car will go quickly."

Then followed many words to convince me of the truth
and urgency of their request.

"When you have brought the money we will go," I said.

The seven-mile trip followed a camel trail through fields
of cotton and corn. The old Chevy "Suburban" lurched
and jounced, inching its way along. The sun blistered. A
fine dust lazed in through the windows.

"You will have to stop here." The policeman broke
the silence. "There is no path from here on. We will
have to walk about a mile yet."

I pulled the car under some thorn trees, found a spot to

stretch out to read my *Time* magazine and to guard the car, while the five shambled off in the glare.

For three hours I lay there reading, dozing, and shifting my nest to keep in the sketchy bit of shade.

To keep a boarding school for eighty boys running smoothly in Somalia, many people were needed. Besides the three Somali teachers and the missionary-director family, there was a gardener, a young man to live with the boys (as something of a father), a cook, a baker, a man to wash the clothes, another one to iron, a man to haul water, a day guard, and a night guard.

There were problems enough in keeping the eighty boys out of one's hair, the neighbors' gardens, and the crocodile-infested river, but the nastiest problems arose between the employees. Many of their fall-outs seemed childish. The man who ironed the schoolboys' clothes accused the washerman of overstarching their khaki shorts so as to make them difficult for him to iron. The cook would accuse the baker of making poor bread so the boys would grumble about the food. The baker blamed the cook for purchasing dirty flour so the bread wouldn't rise. If anything was stolen, the day guard blamed it on the night guard, and vice versa. The dormitory father harassed the water hauler to keep more and fresh water in the barrels for the boys' bathing.

Eventually all the problems had to be brought to me, since I was the acting director, and would judge unbiasedly.

However, I had one handicap. I could not understand the language sufficiently to even begin to catch the heated words. One of the teachers always acted as an interpreter. It was several weeks before I discovered that I was getting a slanted version on all the problems. The teacher

34

obviously had his likes and dislikes on the various disputes, and had people he would like to see being reprimanded. When he would translate the accusations of the various parties, he would give me his version of what was going on, rather than a literal translation. Eventually I caught on.

Among the three teachers, two nearly always sided against Hassan. Generally, I did too. Yet Hassan seemed never to mind the accusations brought against him publicly by the other two teachers when we would attempt to have a teachers' meeting. Usually he would be quiet, urging on a hangdog expression of martyrdom. Occasionally the three would switch sides, with Hassan and the other one siding against my English translator-teacher.

Local elections were being held at Mahaddei and Johar. Quite naturally, Hassan was riding a self-created wave of importance. The other two teachers came from more distant villages. The local election meant nothing to them. Again Hassan had requested to be let off from his teaching for several days to help count votes at Johar.

"Someday, Mr. Hassan, you will have to decide if you are a politician or a teacher," I commented, after hearing his lengthy request and explanation.

"If you are a politician," I continued, "we will fire you; if you are a teacher, we'll probably keep you."

He looked at me morosely.

"You have a hot stomach," he said dryly.

"You may go to Johar. I will take your classes."

When the other teachers saw me in his classroom the next morning, they glanced over me coolly.

At noon, when the boys had dashed off to dinner and a siesta, the other two teachers came to my house.

"Is it peace?" I asked, when they had settled in chairs around me.

"We have come to complain," they said, avoiding my inquiry.

"Must you give all the favors to Hassan?"

"Is he a teacher? No, not even a poor one."

"Why do you keep him?"

"He is ignorant, shouts at the children, and beats them."

"He it is that is always carrying tales against the mission to the village."

"And I will tell you why he wants to go to Johar so much; he has another wife there!"

"Do you pay him when he does not work?"

"Why must you do his work? Mr. Wesselhoeft would not allow this."

The words were all theirs. I did not attempt to answer, for they kept jumping subjects.

"I have nothing to say," I finally inserted, "except one word. Ever since I came here you three teachers have caused more trouble than all the students. You feel that I am new and ignorant, that I am afraid of you, that I am soft. You take advantage of me because I am very young. Had I white hair, you would all listen to me, even Hassan."

They laughed, grudgingly, but quickly recovered their scowls.

"But as it is," I continued, "I am constantly being tested to see what is my strength and what possibly will eventually make me snap. The other night I turned this whole job of running the boys' boarding school over to God. He is going to run it from now on. You can't break me."

They looked at me, puzzled, not fully comprehending the turn of the conversation.

"You see, it's like this," I said. "These first days I was trying to run the school by myself. But I soon learned that the problems were bigger than I could cope with. So I told God that I was sorry to trouble Him, but that He had better lend me a hand, for things were beginning to bump along pretty badly. You know what happened?" I asked, pausing a moment. "Things got worse," I said. "So, I said, 'Okay, God, it's all yours. You take it from here. . . .' "

A commotion on the veranda interrupted our little conversation. About half of the schoolboys had gathered outside the door and were calling for me to come out.

"That old cook gave us a terrible dinner."

"Instead of our regular *pasta,* he gave us. . . ."

"And it had little bugs in it!"

"We are hungry!"

"We are sick!"

"We will die!"

The last remark brought gales of laughter from the older boys. And they took up the cry again.

"We will die!" they whined, holding their stomachs.

"We will die!" the little fellows screeched, rolling on the ground, feigning distress and madness.

"The tea was river water!"

"The meat from a hyena!"

"Even the mangoes were rotten!"

"We are hungry. We are sick. We will die!"

"Quiet! Now stop all this noise!" I shouted, pretending to be angry. "The food is good."

Again yells and boos.

"If anyone is sick and dying, I will go for the clinic boy and he will give each of you a big glass of castor oil!"

They dashed off then, laughing among themselves about castor oil.

"Boys will be boys," I said, turning back to the house. "And teachers, teachers!"

37

Chapter Four

Hippopotami

"Ma'alim! Ma'alim!"

I woke with a jump and thrashed in the dark to rid my-self of the mosquito net. Someone scratching on the screen called, "Teacher! Teacher! There's a hippo! Come quickly!"

Grabbing a bathrobe, I dashed for the door. Nur, the night watchman, was jabbering excitedly.

"He's in the garden. Follow me! I have a torch."

We crept through the bushes. Nur intermittently spotted the light for the briefest second.

"Listen," he hissed.

"What?" I whispered.

"He's eating. You hear?"

"What's he eating?" I asked, when I caught up with Nur at the edge of the cornfield.

"My maize, all my poor little maizes!" Nur whimpered.

I giggled. "Do you see his tracks?" I asked.

Nur flashed the light again.

"There!" I whispered, pointing to the round, flat holes.

But Nur was not seeing the hippo tracks. He saw only his corn plants, mangled, bitten off at the root, and trampled into the ground.

"My maize. My little maize plants!"

"Of course, silly," I said. "Hippos like to eat young corn plants."

"But do you see? They are all hurt!"

But I was not seeing. I had giggled to myself when I thought what a great tale it would make in a letter to friends back home in Lancaster. Running in a bathrobe behind a little man through a cornfield hunting for a hippo in the middle of an African night! I chuckled again to myself.

"Is it so funny?" Nur hissed.

"Sorry—too bad about the corn. But hurry! I want to see a hippo!"

Finding the tracks again with the flashlight, we ran quickly toward the river. Now Nur flashed the light from bush to bush, knowing we were nearing the hippo. Suddenly, with piglike grunts, a heavy shadow lumbered through the open space and slid down the bank to the river.

"Ahaa! I've seen my first, real wild hippo! You're a good tracker, Nur!"

One final gurgle from the direction of the river and then silence folded back over the night in Somalia.

I had just finished up my first year's work in Mogadiscio when the director said, "Omar, pack your oldest clothes and head for the bush country. You're to relieve Wesselhoefts at the boys' boarding school for one month."

I had driven the old "Suburban" the seventy miles north to the boys' school at Mahaddei, a small village of stick houses stacked along the Shebeli River.

"Any hippos in here?" I had asked Nur that first night as we stood together on the bank of the Shebeli staring at the swirling brown water.

"*Ha!*" he replied, using the Somali word for "yes."

"If you see a hippo, yell for me—I've never seen one—except in a zoo."

"But they come in the dark nights when there is no moon. How shall you see when you sleep?"

"But in the daytime. . . ?"

"No, in the day you see a hippo head on the water or his back in the sun—but that is all."

"Are there many hippos in this river?"

"Oh, sometimes they come in big families, fifteen, twenty. Now that the rains have come and the Shebeli is getting big, they will come down the river again from Ethiopia. But you can only see four or five at this place. It is too near a village."

"But I haven't even seen *one,*" I insisted. "If I am sleeping, wake me. If I am teaching the men in the night class, call me. I want to see a hippo. Okay?"

"Okay, *Ma'alim,*" Nur grinned as he attempted the American idiom, but hurriedly added the respectful word for teacher.

Evening was moving among the tall dark grasses when we returned to the veranda.

"The rains have finally come, haven't they?" I said.

"Yes, the rains come and with them long grass and fat cows and much milk," Nur chuckled.

"And much water in the Shebeli," I added.

"And much water in the Shebeli," Nur echoed.

"Remember the hippos, Nur."

"*Ha, Ma'alim.*"

Night stepped from the bush to the open compound, and then quietness. Nur picked up his heavy stick, wrapped his long skirt more tightly about him, and started off on his first round of checking locked doors at the school. I turned to my dark house to light a lantern, and to spend my first night alone in the bush. It was a week later that Nur called me to come see the hippo.

Somalia is a little lowland country tacked on that edge of northeast Africa commonly known as "the Horn." I used to write to my friends back in the States, "You name it, this place probably doesn't have it!" But that was the first year, before I met hippos at the other end of a corn row in my garden. They were my conversion. "This place does have something after all!" I wrote home.

Through the gently undulating grassy plains that slope south to the Indian Ocean, wide green ribbons of tropical plants and cornfields border the brown waters of the She-beli. It's an old river, gathering quickly from the Ethiopian highlands and then slowly flowing its way southeast to Mogadiscio. There it turns suddenly southwest and follows behind the coastal sand dunes until it loses itself in sand and swamp, never quite making it to the ocean. It is a deep river in the rainy season, spilling over its banks here and there. The vegetation that surrounds it is a natural hippo habitat.

There was just such vegetation surrounding the river that lay a hundred yards from the headmaster's house. He had carved a tract for gardening out of the bushland, and had dug a ditch for irrigating. More was cleared than he could handle. He had permitted the Somali workmen to plant their corn gardens in the remainder of the plot. These gardens attracted the hippos, when they finally discovered them.

The hippos looked for the easiest place to come ashore

for their nightly visits. There was such a place, free of bush and with a gently sloping bank, only several hundred feet from the boys' dormitory. The smaller youngsters and those who were born in the city and villages away from river life had an unbelievably absurd fear of being eaten by the hippos.

"But, Mr. Eby," the little boys cried, "you must shoot the hippos. . . ."

"I most certainly will do nothing of the sort," I cut in flatly. "They may be big, but they never attack people."

"But the hippos will eat us in the night."

"Oh, run along, you silly boys. Hippos eat grass."

They left my office, but sat on the veranda beneath the office window, talking in English.

"I suppose he wants us to be eaten!"

"So there would be less of us to teach, no doubt."

"Perhaps he is afraid of the hippo, too!"

"Perhaps he does not know how to shoot a gun."

"Or maybe he is afraid to shoot."

"Oh, no! He is an Americano, and he has a big gun. And all Americanos shoot big guns. Do you not remember seeing them in the cinema?"

"But, they only shoot Indians."

"Of course, silly. The hippo is an African animal."

"Ah, then indeed he is afraid of it!"

I had endured enough. "Get to your classes immediately," I growled through the screen window over their heads.

They fled then, laughing among themselves at having provoked the headmaster.

But the Somali workmen did not indulge in pleasant banter when they discovered that morning after morning the hippos had been out during the night eating their two-foot-high corn plants.

"Shoot the hippos!" they clamored.

"Do not blame me," I said, evading their demand. "I do not guard your corn gardens at night. It is Nur who is always asleep on the job."

Nur's stormy face supplied the challenge to that accusation. "And if I sit in the maize gardens all night, who will watch your house, or the school?"

"Shoot the hippos!" they clamored again.

"But, I can't," I began, trying to win them by pleading with them. "My hunting license does not permit me to shoot any animals larger than the kudu."

They stared at me with sullen eyes.

"I believe you fellows want to see me go to jail," I said, now trying to humor them.

"But the police gave the other headmaster permission to shoot the hippos to keep them away from the dormitories and the gardens. And he didn't have a hippo license either."

"How do I know this is true? He did not tell me. I have no paper saying it."

The men murmured among themselves. A few of them shifted about on their bare feet.

"But, Mr. Eby," Nur began, "our maize. . . ."

"I won't shoot! One of you'll just have to stay up at night and guard the cornfields," I said and stalked to the house. But I read their thoughts. I held the power to protect their gardens but was proving a traitor to them.

A few nights later while I was in the school, Nur dashed in breathlessly.

"He's at it again!" he panted.

"Who's at what again?"

"The hippo. He's in the garden . . . eating much maize. Come, Mr. Eby. Shoot!"

"I will come, but I will *not* shoot!"

"But, Mr. Eby, the hippo, he is very big, and he eats very big. He eats all my little maize. I pray you," Nur begged, "please come and shoot."

For a moment I wanted to shriek ugly words at Nur. I was angry with the men. They would never take "No" for an answer. I had been sent here to run a school for a few weeks. Boys I knew how to handle. But hippos were another matter. I could not bring myself to think of shooting one of the blundering hippos. Indeed, I was sorry about the cornfields being ruined, but it was hardly my fault if the men were so stupid as to plant their fields so near to the river. Yet I was afraid the workmen and some of the other men would create trouble in the village for me and the school. Not that they would be hostile, but even their sulking made me edgy. I wanted them to like me. Perhaps they were right. Kill one of the hippos and it would scare the rest of them away for the season.

Disgusted at my own lack of firmness, I finally said limply, "Okay, I'll come . . . and shoot."

I stood for a moment, still not sure about shooting a hippo. "Sorry, you fool, but I'll have to shoot. You're a threat to me," I said to myself.

Having once decided, I sped to the house, grabbed my Winchester 30-06 and hunted for the shells with a flashlight. This was bush-country Africa, with no electricity; I could not take time to light any lamps. Thoughtlessly I tossed the flashlight on the bed and dashed through the kitchen. While slamming the first shell into the chamber, I spilled the entire box on the floor. I dropped on all fours and began mopping the floor in the darkness, still hugging the gun. Finding five shells, I loaded them as I burst through the back door.

I followed Nur through the night black with no moon.

We slunk along, Nur gripping the darkened flashlight, and I clutching the cold steel of the gun.

"When the light speaks, you shoot," Nur instructed in a whisper.

We crept on.

Suddenly Nur threw on the light.

"Shoot!" he commanded.

I could see nothing. The light was too weak.

"There," Nur pointed. The light fell on the brief outline of a clump of bushes.

"But it is a bush," I protested.

"No, no bush. Hippo!"

Thinking that perhaps he meant the hippo was behind the bush, I decided to fire. In the split second of pulling the trigger I remembered thinking that the outline was suggestive of anything—a cow, an elephant, or a bus. At the crack of the rifle there was a loud grunt, followed by a splash simultaneous with a dull thud.

"He falls!" Nur yelled.

I nearly fell, too, not from the kick of the rifle—but from sheer surprise at having hit something so perfectly in the dark when I had secretly connived to shoot high and merely frighten it off.

"Come, it's not dead!" Nur's shouts set me running.

At twenty feet I unloaded the gun into the beast. I was frightened and sprayed the shells thoughtlessly.

I fled to the house to reload. Having forgotten Nur's flashlight, I stumbled through the darkness. I threw myself on the kitchen floor, flailing my arms and legs, listening for the clink of scattered shells. Finding five more, I tore back to the scene.

The first shot had only grazed the back, causing the hippo to fall into the irrigation ditch. By the time I returned, it had risen on its forelegs and was thrashing about in the muddy water, bellowing hideously. This time I was a bit more methodical. The hippo threw its head violently from side to side and I was still unable to lodge a bullet directly where I thought the brain should be. Standing inches from its head, I blasted the five shells into it.

I ran to the house again for more shells, this time taking the light. When I came back, the policeman and Somali elders from the village were running over the fields to investigate the shots. The fifty-some schoolboys were excitedly dancing around the animal, screaming, and wildly cheering me.

I put two more shells into the head of the hippo. The police, attempting to impress me with their knowledge of big-game hunting, told me not to waste any more shells.

"He will soon die," they said, and spat nonchalantly.

"Yes, he will soon die," Nur echoed.

Inside I was being torn. I was angry over the callous way the men looked on the death of my hippo. And I could not stand its pathetic bellowing in the night. "Die, you fool," I prayed. "Die quickly, please!"

But it did not die quickly. Instead, it heaved about in the few inches of water and mud, its bellows changing to more plaintive bawls.

I was angry at the mob congratulating me, whistling and slapping me on the back and yelling, "Bravo!" I felt sick and wanted to be alone with my sin against the animal. I turned to the schoolboys and blistered them.

"Get to bed, immediately! All of you," I barked.

The hippo ceased bawling and slumped in the mud.

"Yes, it'll stay there overnight. But I'll have to move it early in the morning. No, I'm not proud of my accomplishment." I turned from the villagers and shuffled off toward the house. The act of killing an animal—such a large, helpless animal—seemed to me somehow to be an evil for which there could be no absolution.

I heard the cook stoking the charcoal fires the next morning. He greeted me with obsequious awe in his voice.

"What are all those people doing out there?" I asked while gazing through the window.

"They have come to see your hippo, sir!"

"*My* hippo!"

People were filing in a steady stream to and from my backyard to view the dead animal. Many of the people had never seen hippos; so explained the cook. They had often watched their heads and backs floating above the water, but here, they could inspect one thoroughly!

"Hold the breakfast. Before I eat, I'm pulling that hippo out into the bush!"

"Yes, sir," the cook replied gleefully, and tagged along to watch.

I backed the Volkswagen station wagon over the already badly mangled corn crop to the rear of the hippo. A Somali workman tied the one end of the rope about the axle, profusely cleared his throat and head, and spat on the dead animal. The crowd laughed, but I was puzzled.

"Why?" I asked in Somali. "Why spit on it?"

"It is a pig," Nur said bitterly. "A dirty river pig!"

"No. It's no pig," I began to protest. "Actually, it's a river horse."

The old men scoffed and the students jeered.

"So that's why you wanted me to shoot the hippo, because it is a pig!" Slowly it entered my mind that since they considered the hippo to be a river pig, no wonder they wanted it shot, no wonder they wouldn't touch it, and no wonder they had spat on it, for their Muslim cleanliness recoiled at the mere thought of a pig.

As if reading my thoughts, Nur quickly said, "We wanted it dead because it eats much maize." But I caught a slight gleam in Nur's eyes.

Before I could step into the muddy irrigation ditch, one of the "unbelievers," as his pagan tribe and I were referred to, jumped in and tied the rope about the hippo's leg.

I growled the motor and jounced over the corn ridges, taking up slack in the rope. But the wagon could not budge the hippo. The spinning rear wheels raised clouds of dust. I tried backing up and getting speed, but again, nothing but a neck-breaking lurch and the unhappy whine of the tires.

"Ho! The hippo is indeed a big pig. He has eaten too much of my maize!" Nur sneered. He was in a righteous mood, playing the moment with pompous vengeance, rallying his villagers into gloating over the fate of the helpless, blundering hippo. Boys snickered among themselves, poking indecently at its body with sticks. Ho! It was indeed a time of sporting!

I was angry and scolded the villagers and students for mocking and making sport of a dead body. They only laughed.

An Arab from the village saw his chance for some early business and offered to bring his lorry, the only other vehicle in the village. He would pull the hippo away—for a price. A deal was hurriedly agreed upon.

He brought his lorry and tied up the hippo. The crowd of several hundred villagers, who had gathered to "worship," broke out into wild cheers as the animal was pulled away to the bush.

I turned to the house to drink coffee—strong, black coffee, and to count the days on the calendar till I could return to Mogadiscio civilization where I would sell my gun.

Chapter Five

Mud

A light rain during the night had settled the dusty side streets of Mogadiscio. The morning air, sweeping in through the now opened windows and doors, was fresh with rain scent.

"As badly as Somalia needs her bits of rain," Uncle Clayton began cautiously, "it's still an unwelcome sign for us at least."

Uncle Clayton echoed our thoughts as we all climbed to the flat house roof to scan the early morning sky, hoping to get some clue to the day's further activities.

Roy Shirk had returned to Mogadiscio from a trip south to Margherita. He was hoping to transfer the last of the building supplies and equipment before the rains had completely ruined the roads. But the lesser rains which moved up the coast seemed to have waited until the middle of November. Suddenly, the low skies, black and churning, unloaded in straight walls of rain.

Shirk was still in the city making arrangements for a small load of lumber and several tons of cement to follow later. Now the road to Margherita would be completely impassable, particularly for vehicles without four-wheel drive. The old mission truck, a ton-and-a-half Chevy, seemed to lose its head on bad roads and would churn away, burying itself in a shower of mud.

"Whata ya say we leave about ten o'clock? Give the sun a chance to dry up a bit of mud." Shirk was pressing for an attempt. He had already been stranded in Mogadiscio for two weeks. His wife and family were in Margherita; there also was his work. Sitting around in the city he became restless. He was a man strung together for action only. "But I don't like those ol' cloud heads gathering there in the southwest."

"That sun's really hot this morning," said Uncle Clayton, shielding his eyes and gazing out over the ocean.

"This humidity bugs me!" I said, starting down the steps.

So we left at ten. According to the calendar it was Thanksgiving Day in the United States, but I was not being particularly thankful. For some time I had hinted that I should take a visit to see the lower end of Somalia, the Margherita and Chisimaio region. My chance had come, but not as I had particularly wanted it to.

Uncle Clayton and I were going along with Shirk to Margherita to bring back one of the mission cars. Mogadiscio had not had any for several weeks. Both of us were going because we knew the conditions of the roads.

The first twenty kilometers of macadam road lay ahead. Here and there little pockets of shiny black marked pools of water which had collected from the night's rain. The camel trains and thorn trees whirled by quickly. Then suddenly we made a sharp turn and left the tar road. A few kilometers further would have brought us to the village of Afgoi, which lay among her fields of produce. But we were heading south. And the only road south was a dirt one, though now it was mud.

Two roads run south from Mogadiscio. Though one is more legendary than real, the other could well be named "Somalia, Route 1 South." But that is being too pretentious; there is only one road south from Mogadiscio, except, of course, the legendary route.

During the rainy season the roads were closed—or rather, barricades of barrels, pipes, rails, and locks suggested that they were closed. These dirt roads were dusty during the dry seasons, but mud and stretches of water when it rained. The roads were worn down lower than the sides; thus much of the water drained on to them.

The legendary road was known as the Sand Dune Road. During the dry season the road did not exist. It was as impossible as "Somalia Route 1 South" in the rainy season. A car would sink into the dry, powdery, orange and beige sands. But during the rainy season, the Sand Dune Road came to life, when the sands, heavy with moisture, would pack into a hard trail, generally.

Always the Somalis would refer to the road as being "over there." Usually one was lucky if he could stumble upon it. It was only a trail that wound in and out among red sandy hills. The hills were old, old sand dunes slowly becoming conditioned to support some scrubby thorns and sharp-bladed sand grass. At the foot of the hills, the good rich loam sloped away to the right of the road. The road found this soil line and held it for the hundred or more kilometers that the red sand hills humped south. Always the road stayed on the sands, a little beyond the reach of the loam which had now turned into a quagmire of muck. Already the bright green blades of maize and the dull green leaves of cotton plants dotted the soil.

To the left the sandy hills piled one over another, softly curving upward till one never quite knew when he was at the top. On the other side, the hills stretched out gently till they lost themselves in the sand of the seashore. There, just over the edge of these hills, the Indian Ocean, dark and oily, pounded away on the beach.

Now we were riding along on the Sand Dune Road. It was rough going. The truck jounced over tightly packed mounds of sand. It lurched and pitched as we crept along, seldom going above ten or fifteen miles per hour, and most of the time in second gear.

It was my turn to drive. The old Chevy handled like a tank. We lunged around a bend and there, right in front of us, was a lorry slouched in mud in the middle of the road. This was bad. But what made it worse was the fact that water was flowing in ditches at both sides of the road.

"Keep movin'!" Shirk yelled and leaped from the truck.

A scramble from the back told me that the Somali men who had been riding there had also jumped from the truck. The road was high in the middle and sloped sharply to the ditches. Shirk and his Somali men had run along the side of the truck and were pushing on it to keep it from slipping into the ditch as we spun along, slinging mud and weaving giddily.

"Whew! We made it through!" Shirk gasped as he slid into the truck.

Ahead of us the road straightened out. We could see pond after pond of water.

"Don't slow down for any of them," Shirk instructed. "If there is water in them, then they must have solid bottoms. Otherwise, most of the water would have drained off and they would be deep mudholes."

He was right. But I found myself by natural instinct wanting to ease up on the speed as we approached each pond.

Sometime later, in attempting to pass another lorry stranded in the middle of the road, I gently slid the truck into the ditch. No amount of pushing, spinning, cutting of small trees and stuffing them under the tires, or jacking up the rear end would help. Finally, we took down shovels from the truck and opened a path for the tires to follow, all the while stuffing under them small tree branches for them to grip.

"I'll drive now for a while," Shirk said rather wearily, and we eased off down the road.

We hadn't gone more than a half hour when we came to a huge pool of water stretching for acres across both sides of the road. Shirk attempted to go right through it since there was no path to turn out and go around it. We sprayed water for about a hundred yards and then suddenly the motor gave one cough and stopped.

We sat in that hole an hour and a half. We all slipped off our shoes and went to have a look under the hood.

"It must be something greater wrong than just drowned out." Shirk moaned softly, for he had just dried all the spark plugs and had attempted to start the engine; but there was no response.

Uncle Clayton offered all the suggestions he could. Recognizing my mechanical ineptitude, I didn't offer a suggestion. Perhaps my silence proved just as annoying.

After an hour of helping Shirk wiggle, unscrew, and screw every item under the hood, Uncle Clayton and I waded to the bank.

"May as well play some chess!" Uncle Clayton suggested, and produced his tiny portable chess set, no bigger than a man's hand.

We had not made too many moves when Shirk came up from under the hood for air. With mouth hanging, he stared at us in utter disbelief. This was his last straw! But he did little more than groan brokenly and go back to riddling under the hood.

"Of all things!" he mumbled.

"Have to keep Omar's mind from thinking about staying out here in the bush with the hyenas all night," Uncle Clayton said, interpreting the moans and mutters coming from under the truck hood.

Speaking for myself, I replied, "I am not frightened at all. But we are miles from any village or civilization. How can we get help?"

It was five o'clock when we pulled from the muddy lake. Shirk did not know what happened, but when he had gone to try the motor again, it started. Perhaps it was the combined efforts of our prayers. In any case, Shirk wanted to go on—so on we went—for two miles. In the middle of the road, with water flowing on both sides, another lorry was stranded. That was our Waterloo! We had been on the road for seven and a half hours and were still only one fourth of the way to Margherita.

We turned around there and headed back to Mogadiscio, bouncing and spraying muddy water for another five hours. It was ten o'clock in the night when we pulled into the mission compound at Mogadiscio. We had been on the road for twelve hours. Thanksgiving Day was about over, and I had found something for which to be thankful!

Two weeks later we received a telegram from Margherita telling us that the roads were now open.

The three of us left Mogadiscio again, early in the morning. The sun was bright and we thought the day to be ours. As far as the village, Genali, or for the first three hours, things weren't too bad. We were traveling on the main road, but a light rain had passed, turning its surface to mud as slippery as ice.

Once again we had to find our way over to the Sand Dune Road in order to continue. The road was very much like it was two weeks earlier. We lurched along for hours. Then suddenly we sank into mud. The truck was stranded, mud up to the axle and no traction.

We sat in that hole for nearly two hours. We tried jacking up the rear of the truck to stuff branches under the wheels, but the jack kept sinking into the mud. We would dig out the mud, stuff in more branches, dig loose more mud and stuff more branches, and move forward a few feet. All this under the blazing afternoon sun. Finally, a bulldozer from a nearby Italian banana plantation happened along and pulled us free.

It was five o'clock and we were halfway. The road was barred; a Somali policeman sat under a baobab guarding the barricade.

"Won't let anyone through that doesn't have the permission of the district commissioner," Shirk announced. He had returned to the truck after having spoken with the guard.

"So that means we have to go over the hill to Brava to the D.C.'s office and get permission."

We were at a junction. The Sand Dune Road had dumped us back on to the main road. The seacoast village of Brava lay over the red hills to the east. There was nothing to do but go there and plead our case.

Surprisingly we spent little time in securing permission. Perhaps the D.C. had fears of having to find us Europeans housing in his village if he would refuse us permission to continue. Nevertheless, we were soon on the road again. Before leaving, we had telegraphed our mission friends at

Margherita telling them we were at Brava and were heading south and requested them to come after us.

Shirk handed the Somali policeman our slip of paper from the D.C.'s office. He took it, read it carefully, or at least made his lips move, and gave a big nod of approval. He unlocked the gate and swept us through with a great ostentatious gesture.

All the while the policeman was pretending to be reading the permission slip, he was holding the paper upside down! But what a show! He didn't falter the slightest; his hand was steady and his face had the complacent look of a job well executed.

We were rolling along in high spirits, not hitting too many mudholes. Night had come in quickly, as it always did so near to the equator. It was indeed a strange thing to travel at night through desert country, now pushing with green buds because of the rains. All was flat and black. The constant roar of the truck was the only disturbance on the night air. Had we stopped for a few minutes we would have observed how thick the quietness of an African night really was. Yet it really wasn't quiet. The yapping of the nocturnal animals, the twittering of the bush birds, and the drilling of the millions of insects all blended in a swell of small praise. Those sounds were a part of the night. And when one became accustomed to an African night, the presence of those small noises was not so noticeable as their absence. Yet an African night was quiet—frightening, menacing, awesome.

The white lights of the truck cut a swath through the black bush. But behind the truck darkness snapped back. There where the trees were all momentarily alight, now darkness enshrouded them again.

Uncle Clayton was driving. Shirk and I were dreaming

our own weary thoughts. On the back, Roy's right-hand man, Abucar, sat wrapped in a blanket dozing.

"Look out! We're gonna hit it!" Uncle Clayton was shouting, his dignity completely shattered.

There in the path of the truck lights lay the biggest old mudhole we had ever seen. With one slam of the pedal, Uncle had discovered that the brakes had given way. It all happened so quickly. The next moment we were sliding off the road into a dreadful ditch of mud.

Stuck, and a repeat performance of cutting branches, stuffing them under the rear tires, digging mud, and the crazy singing of the spining tires, but this time all was done in the darkness.

The whine of the motor announced on the still night air that some stupid Europeans were stranded. A free show for a good laugh. We had been working for almost an hour when a group of young Somali men and girls crashed through the bush, nudging and laughing and calling to each other. We asked them to all join in and give us a push. We even offered money. But this was night, and their work was ended, and here were three silly Americans, mud-splattered and ridiculously stranded. Ho! This was indeed a night for sporting!

We turned back with bitter hearts to our routine of cutting branches and stuffing them under the tires, of pushing first forward and then backward, rocking and spinning.

Finally, when three of the Somali men saw that we were in earnest about getting out of the hole, they stepped up and lent their muscles. The six of us pushing, with Uncle Clayton at the wheel, soon got us back on to the road. Darkness, mud, and seventy miles lay ahead. It was nine o'clock.

Thirty miles further we got stuck again. This time for good. It was eleven o'clock and not a person around. The only noises one could hear were the grunting of the wild hogs and frogs and the buzzing of millions of mosquitoes.

Roy and Abucar decided they would walk on to the nearest village, Gelib. Clayton and I settled down to battle the mosquitoes. We buttoned our collars and sleeves, covered our hands and faces, closed the truck windows, and promptly broke out into a fainty sweat. We had to have air, so we opened the windows again, and in came the mosquitoes.

I seemed to be losing all sense of time. Shirk returned after what I thought to be a few minutes later, but it was actually three hours since he had left. The twenty-five miles to Gelib was proving to be too far for as tired as he was. Abucar decided to go on and secure help at Gelib. Even so, he would probably not arrive there until early morning.

With the return of Shirk we three decided to try once more to get the truck out. For another hour we repeated the day's formula of pushing, rocking, shoveling mud, and stuffing sticks under tires. It was now three o'clock in the morning, and we decided to get some sleep. We let Uncle Clayton have the soft truck seat among the swarming mosquitoes for his bed. Shirk and I stretched out on the metal roof that covered the bed of the truck. A canvas served as a blanket. There was one blessing. We were too high to be bothered with many mosquitoes.

Morning brought one of the loveliest sunrises I had ever seen. A flush of rose and green washed the eastern sky.

Now thirst and hunger were among us. We decided we would have to ration our drinking water to make it last for the second day. The meal that was packed for yesterday's dinner was now also serving as breakfast of the next morning.

At nine in the morning a jeep came from the D.C.'s

office at Gelib. As it was impossible for him to pull us out, we went with him to the village.

We still had an hour's drive to Margherita. The men from the mission were not coming. Something must be wrong. So we rented a jeep and headed for Margherita. About three fourths of the way there we met Victor Dorsch and Chester Kurtz coming for us. The telegram that we had sent at five o'clock the evening before had finally reached them at eleven-thirty the next day.

There in the middle of the road, fifteen minutes from our destination, we turned about and headed back to our stranded truck.

Returning the borrowed jeep in Gelib, we traveled on in the mission LandRover. With us in the vehicle were eight Somalis who had been hired to come along and push.

Now at the stranded truck we proceeded to unload the lumber and small equipment. Twice we had to do this. An Italian in a jeep equipped with chains had come out to inspect the road. He offered the aid of his vehicle when he saw our plight.

So we hooked the jeep and the LandRover to the truck, which was now emptied. Twelve of us men pushed. Slowly the old Chevy came out of the mud and on to drier road.

Now we had to drive wildly. In the west, black clouds were moving in angrily and Margherita lay an hour away. We arrived—thirty-eight hours after we had left Mogadiscio, a trip that normally took six hours.

Chapter Six

English

I walked into my classroom the first day a few minutes before class was scheduled to meet. Most of the students were already at their desks. As I entered the room, there was a scraping of chairs being pushed back from the desks. The class stood up and remained standing until I said, "Good afternoon," and sat down. Then they sat down and continued looking over their lessons or papers or whatever they had out to occupy their time until class began.

The first day this happened I interpreted it as a generous gesture on their part in recognizing their new teacher. I had inherited the class from Uncle Clayton. But when they popped to their feet the next day and the next, not only in this class, but in the other classes which I had taken over from Uncle, I inquired of him why they did this.

"It's the way they always did to me, too. I assumed it must be done in the public Italian schools, as a gesture of respect," explained Uncle Clayton.

"But I don't like it. Such a display embarrasses me. It always takes me a few minutes to gain composure before I can take up the lessons. I think I am going to suggest to them that they drop it."

Later I expressed to the class my appreciation for the respect they showed me as a teacher. We talked about it, they expressing why they did it and I telling them how I felt. Finally, I suggested that I would understand they still respect my position as a teacher even if they would discontinue the practice of snapping to attention whenever I walked into the room.

"After all," I concluded, "most of you students are men older than I, and young people are to show respect to elders. So, in that you are older than I am, and I have a bit more education than you, this should make us about equal, so that you do not have to stand in my presence, or bow to me."

They smiled and some chuckled at my reasoning, but the class settled noticeably into a more relaxed atmosphere.

Friends frequently wrote to me asking how I could possibly be teaching English as a foreign language without knowing any of the country's languages: Arabic, Somali, Italian, and Swahili. The first several weeks with a class of beginners were never easy, sometimes almost despairing. I was glad that no one could watch me teach, except those who were my students, and they really wanted to learn.

Among the educational cliques of that time the current cliché named my method "The Direct Method." But educators revamp their vocabularies every three to five years, so that by now the method may be known by a completely different piece of jargon. In any case, English was the only language used in the teaching situation. I never resorted to their vernacular, except for those rare occasions when communication completely broke down. For many of the nouns I used pictures, illustrations from books and magazines, or my own line drawings. Verbs were acted out. Adjectives of color, size, number, and degree could easily be demonstrated, as could most simple adverbs. Soon a vocabulary of very concrete terms was built up. On this foundation, the lessons branched out into more complex sentence structures and more abstract vocabularies. It was always the abstract qualities which stumped me; for how could one act out "love," "sympathy," or "honor"?

One of the classes which I took over from Uncle Clayton when I arrived was well advanced in their study of the English language. Wilbert Lind had had them for years prior to Uncle Clayton. It was this class that was the most interesting to teach in those early months of my job. They were studying a simple English literature book. Of course, they didn't know Shakespeare from Milton and T. S. Eliot. In fact, they weren't personally acquainted with Tom Sawyer or Huck Finn. But poetry didn't have to rhyme or march along iambically to be poetry. That they knew!

"What shall I tell my friends in America about you?" I asked this advanced class one time.

"Tell them we like English!" they unanimously offered.

Then I remembered. Another teacher had asked her class in America a similar question. But they discouragingly volunteered a different answer. "Tell them we hate English!"

Quite a contrast, isn't it? We, who have been born amid the babble of English, brand the encounter with demonstrative pronouns or dangling modifiers as impossible. Yet

62

the foreign student will attack subjunctive conditionals and idiomatic prepositions with gusto.

Surprisingly enough, my students did a fair job. Oh, there was the occasional bungle. For instance, on a test we were making lists of feminines and masculines, when one of the students wrote that "cow" was the masculine of "hen." Another time a student negatively replied to my question as to whether his father had any children.

On another day the beginners were talking about food, cooking, plates, forks, and eating. One young student, in broken English, told me that he was not married and occasionally liked to cook his own meals. This surprised me, for I thought that such a chore would have been beneath his dignity. I talked about it for a while, telling them that I, too, enjoyed working with foods. One old man, not to be left outside the conversation, volunteered, "I have a wife who cooks the food, but sometimes I also like to cook my wife."

When the class broke into wild laughter, he was upset, until someone told him in Somali what he had said in English.

During the earlier days of my teaching I became much concerned about the purpose and function of the school. We were continually being pressured to start more and more classes. They seemed not to realize that there was a limit to what I could get accomplished. Not only were they asking for more English classes; they asked for anything from advanced law to human anatomy. Really, we could have had a Somali Mennonite "College" right there in Mogadiscio.

In that first week I turned away over fifty men who wanted to join my classes. Already I had as many as forty men in a classroom that was built and equipped to accommodate twenty-four. But what could I do? My personal idea was that the English classes were not the end, but only a means to the end. If this was true, then I wanted to keep my classes of such a size that I could deal personally with each student. This I believed was the feeling of the other missionary teachers. But the "mass production English factory" was being pushed on us.

Why all the craze to learn English? One very obvious reason was that the United States Consulate had announced that it would offer approximately fifteen scholarships to Somali students to continue their education in America. Of course, what many of the Somali students did not realize, or more likely, did not stop to take time to find out, was that only those who had completed their secondary education would qualify for the examinations for conferring the scholarships.

All the neighboring countries of Somalia used the English language as either the first national language or as the second. It seemed that Somalia knew if she ever meant to get along with these she would have to use some English with them.

More basically, the interest in English stemmed from the several years that the British governed Somalia during the end of World War II and immediately after it. When the Italians marched into Kenya, they bit off more than they had bargained. Britain soon had her enemy chased back over the border, and pursued her to the ocean. Wherever Britain goes she begins teaching her English language. So, during those years of British occupancy, many Somalis had their first taste of learning the English language.

The Mennonite mission arrived some few years later, after Somalia had been handed back to the Italians to govern under the United Nations. English was still in popular demand.

As a mission we did not care if they learned English or not. That was hardly our primary concern. But we immediately saw that it was an opportunity to contact people, to acquaint them with who we were and discover who the Somali was. Thus we began teaching English.

Slowly this exposure grew into an acquaintance. The acquaintance into a rapport.

The making of classes was necessary and the teaching of English was good, but it really was not enough. The more personal encounter outside of the classroom was far more rewarding. I did not ever expect to see any of my students, while I was explaining relative pronouns, fall to the floor and inquire about what they must do to be saved. Maybe I lacked faith, but seemingly things did not move that way.

Actually the students watched each other like hawks to see if any one of them was giving a favorable ear to anything the "infidel" teacher might slip in about religion, or the Person Jesus, or what it meant to be a Christian. Even the skirting of such subjects was met with a silent wall of watching eyes. For this reason I never began my English classes with prayer, as did some of the other missionaries. It just never seemed appropriate to me.

In Mogadiscio I was teaching at our mission's English night school for adults. Classes generally ran from four o'clock in the afternoon through to nine o'clock at night. Occasionally when I felt that I should be doing more, I would take on an additional class at three o'clock, or add another class to run from nine to ten. But that was during the first year, when I didn't know my own strength, nor that of the hot weather.

Classes were one hour long; at the beginning of each hour, a new class would arrive for its lesson in English. Wilbert Lind taught elementary arithmetic and Bible; Mrs. Lind taught typing and bookkeeping. I taught most of the English lessons.

We conducted a night school in Mogadiscio for the simple reason that most of our students were employed during the day in government offices or shops. Others of our English students were regular secondary students in the government schools during the morning. We adjusted our schedules to aid us in contacting the greatest number of people, for it was people whom we had come to serve, and not they to suit us.

"No school tomorrow, Mr. Eby!" volunteered one small boy, who obviously was attending classes because his father made him.

"And why not?" I asked.

Before he could answer, many of the older students severely hushed him in Somali, and then turned to explain to me that it was an insignificant holiday and that we should have school.

"It's a religious holiday!" he piped in.

Now I was concerned, for we tried to regulate our school with that of the public schools, at least closing when they shut down for religious holidays. If they closed, it would be an important religious holiday.

"The government schools will be closed," he continued.

"What is the holiday in memory of?" I finally got in.

"It is in memory of the day that Abraham was tempted to kill Isaac."

"Also it is the day when Adam came to the earth."

"And Eve, sixty years later."

"Sixty years later!" I repeated, surprised.

"Yes, Adam did not have a wife till he was sixty years

old," they related laughingly. "But he lived to be very old."

"Perhaps we had better declare it a holiday. You all have been working quite hard for the past several weeks."

Just such a small incident as trying to keep me in ignorance concerning their national religious holidays proved again to me how earnest they were about their studies of the English language.

Teaching my native language as a foreign language added an exciting dimension to my own studies of literature and the workings of the English language.

Chapter Seven

Mogadiscio (ii)

We moved a little nearer heaven than we were before—
one hundred feet up, and six city blocks (as Middle East
city blocks run) northwest. The old mission headquarters
rusted and molded away in the apartment flat two hundred yards from the Indian Ocean front and twenty feet
above sea level. So we went up—up on a hill. From my
porch the city skyline from left to right ran something
like this: twin Catholic cathedral towers, blue-glazed
Muslim minaret, the city's one and only smokestack (smog
was no immediate menace), till-midnight-open-seated
theater, black-and-white striped police headquarters, pris-
on towers and walls, cemetery gates and gardens.

Full length on the east, our property bordered the
Somali Fairgrounds. Exactly on the other side of this the
Sudan Interior Mission was located. The fairgrounds
served as something of a "denominational barrier!" Separating us from the people along the street was a stone
fence with two gigantic black iron grille gates; to the
south, a formidable growth of cacti and an eight-foot wall;

to the west, a fifteen-foot hedge, nonpenetrable by the skinniest of donkeys roaming the streets.

Leaving the street and slipping through a small gate in the big iron gates, a person would follow a macadam path up the hill. The total compound struck me immediately as being comparable to a miniature plantation uprooted from the Carolinas or Mississippi and plunked down there in the tight little city. It was lovely! Something like soft, billowy willows stirred and wept with the air. And tall-look-like-pines shook their fingers and tossed inch-long cones. Here and there the flamboyant flared with a bewildering sight of red.

On each side of the walk were two coral stone houses— simple, square, flat-roofed, colonial Italian houses. In the one to the left, an Italian man and his British wife were living; the one to the right—the Wilbert Lind family. Eventually, when we would have more mission workers in the city, the other house could be used as living quarters for them. Further up the hill, sitting in the middle of the compound was the most imposing of the buildings. Oddly enough, here was where I lived (or rather in one small part of it). This was the guesthouse which was to accommodate outstation missionaries when they came to town, and other visitors. The house was built like the others, but it had the most commanding view of the city life and ocean activities.

Directly behind the house was a monstrous block building once used for a tannery. That should probably be named "Wesselhoeft Hall." The Wesselhoeft family had been in the city for two months, during which a small girl was born to them. Carl spent many days working on that old building. The whole building was rewired and lights were hung. One large room was converted into a student recreational facility—ping-pong! And part of the

69

same room was used for a student reading room and library. The other rooms needed cleaning, repairing, and arrangement of storage space. The building had two towers (just like an old castle without a moat). In one of them Mrs. Lind started a typing class for six fellows.

The fifth large building was beside the old tannery. And that should be called "Shirk Hall." Roy spent his last month in Somalia supervising and working with a group of Somalis to plaster, paint, and rewire the building. There was one large room in which we had our English worship services on Sunday. Then there were two other large classrooms which Wilbert Lind and I occupied regularly for teaching. Looking down under one of the chapel windows, one could see a "hippopotamusless" hippo pool. There were two of them; both empty. And in the student reading room a massive elephant skull was displayed on the wall.

Having brushed a quick portrait of our city mission, I whispered a dedicatory prayer.

"Oh, God, I again give Thee thanks for a home church that had such vision and interest in Christian mission and for a mission board that had focused a Muslim field before them. Then I thank Thee for the home church that approved the purchasing of such spacious facilities. Lord, it was more than we missionaries dared hope or ask. We just give it back to Thee and ask that Thou wouldst continue to teach us how to use it.

"For something green in this desert, and a few red buds —for this our little mission oasis, I give Thee thanks. May the weary turn aside and find rest under our trees, the thirsty, a cup of cold water, and the students, Lord, let them find knowledge, particularly of Thy Son, the Lord Jesus. Teach us to open our houses and our hearts to all these people that in the unrehearsed staging of programs and life they might see only Jesus. Bless all who enter this place. Amen."

There's one little story of Mogadiscio life I seldom tell— attending the Fourth of July parties at the American Consulate.

I was in the country during two July Fourths and attended both parties. There was nothing very unusual about that. The Consulate invited any Americans that happened to be in the city over that date. There was an American community of several hundred living in Somalia: the various oil exploration concerns, the foreign aid office, as well as the overstaffed American Consulate. Many of these were in Mogadiscio.

There was nothing unusual about my attending the parties (although I seldom tell it, because of my weaker brethren); the other Mennonite missionaries went, too.

It would indeed be odd for the whole lot of us tee-totalers to accept invitations to such a party were it not for one thing. Many top Somali government officials were invited. Now a good Muslim will not drink alcoholic beverages, for the Koran forbids it. At least this much must be said for the American government representatives in Somalia: they had the sense to serve many kinds of nonalcoholic drinks at their parties. And this, plus the fact that one could meet many of the Somali elite, was why we missionaries were attracted. They served imported fruit and vegetable juices, American sweets and hors d'oeuvres, food we hadn't eaten for months, sometimes years.

"More drinks, sir?" asked a Somali waiter in stiff white, extending an immense tray laden with glittering glasses of drinks and juices.

71

I had just eaten an unusually hot-peppered "zamboozie," and was ready for something to cool my mouth.

"Yes, good. I'll take a drink," I said, picking up a glass. The waiter moved on. I took one long swallow. The inside of my head lit up brightly. Something pleasantly warm titillated my throat. What I thought to be a glass of water turned out to be a very dry martini! How naive could I be! To think that they would serve water at a cocktail party!

The room was swirling with people. Any moment now someone who knew me might step by. I almost panicked! I couldn't be caught nursing a martini by some of the other missionaries.

On the other side of the room, great potted palms lined the wall. Nonchalantly I inched my way along the wall around the outside of the group, keeping my eyes alert for any friends. With one last glance about the room, I backed up to a palm tree, lowered the glass behind me, and drained it into the planter.

My breath! Could anyone smell that I had been drinking? I made a headlong charge for the buffet table, and stained my breath with sardines. For one moment I wondered if I might become intoxicated, since I was so terribly pure. Not that I would become drunk, but just high!

"And now, my friends, the President of the United States has recorded a message to his Americans living abroad," the Consul General was speaking. "Let us listen to this recording."

President Eisenhower spoke for a few minutes, praising us Americans for what we were doing abroad. I kept thinking that he should make a tour in disguise among his servants.

"Now let us drink a toast to the Honorable President, Dwight D. Eisenhower."

I lifted high my orange juice glass for a moment, then drained the contents.

"And now, ladies and gentlemen, the national anthem."

It was good to hear the Marine Band playing that music.

"What hymn is that? It sounds familiar to me," a missionary whispered in my ear.

I froze, wondering if any other person heard him ask me. For a fleeting moment I thought he, too, had been drinking!

Through the little apertures of the latticework that ran cater-cornered, to give it less the appearance of bars, I gazed out on a forbidden world. The world was a green one of sloping lawns and sunken gardens and floppy elephant-eared tropical plants. It was a forbidden world, for I had to check twenty-some students' grammar exercises, all on the same theme with mere erroneous variations.

It was twenty to five and that for me was the time of day when in Africa it seemed sacrilegious to do anything but go out of the house and sit in the garden. The glaring three o'clock sun had slipped two more degrees down the western slope. Lacy shadows from the flamboyant trees were being tossed crazily about on the ground, and palm branches with their hundred spiked fingers nodded stiffly. Twenty minutes to five, the time of day when (since I was so unfortunate as to be working) time seemed to stop and the minutes fell the length of years.

Director Lind and his family were vacationing in the Nairobi, Kenya, area for the month. So this meant that I was holding the Mogadiscio fort alone and running the whole show. New to me was the job of dashing about the city buying potassium permanganate, trimicina, and helemezine elixir (medicines probably for dysentery, worms, or syphilis—seems we had little else there) and arranging to send them to our nurses on the outstations.

Then there were the religious services to chew my nails over. While I didn't have the license of a Right Reverend nor any training in homiletics for that matter, I found my calling, teaching, to be of some help.

My congregation was a knee-knocker. The Somalis (bless them, their tribe's attendance increased) were an enjoyable enough group to speak to, but the white American influx who came (I knew not why) destroyed all of my poise. There were the top administrators of the International Co-operative Assistance, Sinclair pilots, consular attaché, technical experts, and others holding just as imposing titles. Remembering what the Lord Jesus had done in my heart and the need to tell of this again and again blessed me with enough courage, however, to conduct services.

I found that nothing very spectacular happened to me upon becoming a missionary, but that I was like others of the mission family. We were all rather common folks— Mennonites with "in the world, but not of the world" problems. And very common things demanded most of the days of my assignment. Common things happened to me, like frying eggs and making coffee, teaching reflexive pronouns and indirect speech, sewing buttons and saying prayers, or hunting the mislaid scissors, or wondering if anyone had missed me enough to write a letter. Oh, there were a few thrilling, red-letter days among all the black ones. Sometimes I even became romantic about my place. Once I tried writing a little poem about all that I saw and a bit of what I felt. It ran something like this:

SOMALIA

Oh, the golden glories of my newfound homeland....
The country plains, the city lanes,
Washed with the monsoon rains,
Lie sheen and glimmer
In a shimmery emerald green.

The blue-green Indian
Rushes in and breaks frothy white
On the miles and miles of cream beaches,
And slaps green finger-waves
Insistently up pinnacled coral,
Black and salt-crystalline.

Evening creeps down, lilac and rose
Over town, and roads, flushing
White-faced finger-slender minarets
And bubble-domed mosques with
African evening hectic reds while
Camel trains file into their trails.

Night steps from the crest of the hills.
Knowing surely the day is safely past,
People breathe back love and life
And pray with sweet ease of relief.

Oh, the golden glories of my newfound homeland....

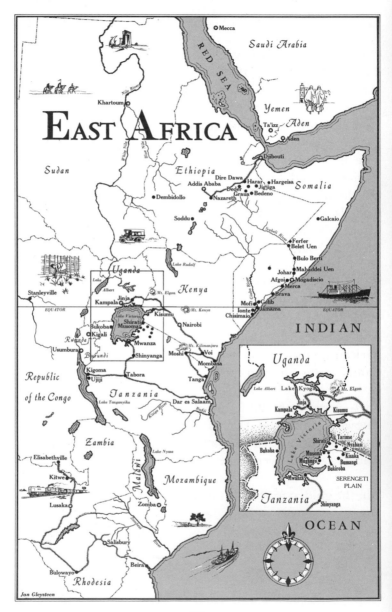

Mogadiscio, capital of Somalia Republic, lacks a proper port. Ocean-going vessels must lie offshore about a mile and be loaded and unloaded by lighters operating from the small harbor protected by a sea wall.

The streets and public buildings of Mogadiscio were colorfully lighted, celebrating the newly achieved independence, July 1, 1960.

Located on a main plaza downtown Mogadiscio, the Roman Catholic cathedral and the mosque dominate the skyline.

Camels and donkeys make up much of Somalia's transport, for most roads are generally impassable to motor vehicles during the rainy seasons. These camels headed toward Mogadiscio along the road Mussolini had built are bringing grass and grain to the markets

In Somalia, the scarcity of water makes it a valuable commodity. After a shower, women collect the rain water.

Seen here at four o'clock in the afternoon, the author, who taught in the mission's English night school for adults, opens the door to his classroom.

I do not know how many trips I made to the airport to see students off. Always my best students were being snapped up for scholarships to Italy, U.S.S.R., England, America, China, and Egypt. For them I was happy. And as often happened, some of my best students were also some of my closest Somali friends, and I would miss them very much.

One large building on the Mogadiscio compound had one large room in which English worship services were conducted, and two smaller rooms, which Wilbert Lind and the author used for English and other classes.

With the ending of my teaching, the inevitable lining up for picture-taking followed. Photography was still such a new thing to Somalia that nothing but the most formal poses were considered acceptable. Casual, informal poses were sacrilegious to the very goddess of photography. So we stood like so many shiny, tin soldiers, with never a smile.

Sitting in the middle of the mission compound was the guesthouse, arranged to accommodate outstation missionaries when they came to town. In part of this house the author lived for a year and a half.

Siestas, that sane institution of the tropics, was not only a time for napping but also for meditating and reflecting.

The road north from Mogadiscio cut straight through the silvery-gray bush, desolate and mysterious.

The author found the motor scooter to be the cheapest and most convenient way to get around downtown. On rare, more daring excursions, the scooter was also used for ventures to the interior.

On a month's holiday safari through other East African countries, the author traveled with the Victor Dorsch family and Allen Brubaker. Here, a pause for lunch under Kenya's spreading trees.

Lions at a kill in the Nairobi Park, Kenya.

On a little knoll under some acacia trees, marked on the map as "Lion Hill," the eye saw only the sweep of the sky and the silent, naked curve of the earth.

Wreath-crowned: a modest declaration that one had made it to the top of Mt. Kilimanjaro. The author, in the middle, is flanked on the right by Maynard Kurtz and on the left by Donald Mellinger.

During the rainy season, the Juba River in southern Somalia runs wide, muddy, and swift.

The Pax fellows at Torda trained oxen and men to work with each other for easier, cheaper soil preparation.

In the bush, beauty and dignity.

At an interior village, cattle file close by a stately mosque with minaret.

Always the donkeys. And they're used for everything—hauling furniture, water, cement, people, grain, dead camels. Often they are abused, too, straining against a load of staggering weight.

Donkeys roam on the outskirts of a small village nestled under a stand of acacia, baobab, and date palms.

Some miles from Mogadiscio, nomads drive their cattle and goats to water at the Shebeli River.

Somalis sell their sheep and goats at an outdoor livestock market.

Chapter Eight

Holidays

We had left hot, barren, desolate Somalia and were headed for the civilization of green Nairobi, Kenya. It was the end of my first year, and the Dorsch ·family, Allen Brubaker, and I had mapped out a month's safari through Kenya, Uganda, and the eastern edge of the Congo. This was the first leg of the journey—overland from Margherita to Nairobi.

Coming to Nairobi fresh from some European city calls for little reason to be bug-eyed. One has to live for a year in a city like Mogadiscio before the awesomeness of Nairobi leaves one a bit breathless.

After loading the little Volkswagen bus with a month's supply of tinned foods, a few days' supply of fresh fruits and vegetables, spare cans of gasoline and water, cots, luggage and a tent, we headed west from Nairobi.

Suddenly, we were on the edge of the great Rift Valley. A panoramic sweep of farming and grazing lands stretched away below us. Again, one must live in a desert for a year to be fully caught up with such a scene. Holstein cows, a railroad, and a combine in a wheat field dumbfounded even me, the least of the agrarian-minded in the car.

We spent the first night under a wet tent at a little place named Equator. Although on the equator, it was miserably cold, for we were 8,715 feet above sea level. Again, one must live at sea level in a hot desert for a year to enjoy the shock of such a change.

All afternoon a thunderstorm rumbled at our backs as we wound through Eldoret and on into Tororo, Uganda. There we stopped at a police station to inquire about a place to pitch our tent for the night. We slept on the lawn beside the station.

Before we left the next day, one of the policemen told us always to ask at a police station in Uganda before pitching a tent.

"They'll never refuse you," he added, as we drove off for Jinja and Kampala.

In Kampala we stopped at the police headquarters, a handsome several-floor building.

"Yes, you can pitch your tent right over there," he said.

We followed his gesture. He pointed to a large open lawn directly across the street. It was a kind of park. Office buildings and apartment flats bordered all sides.

"Isn't there any place that would be a bit more private?" Victor cautiously asked.

They directed us south of the city to another police station.

"There's a place about a mile south of here. The Governor's Lodge. It has a lot of open lawns all around it. You can pitch there. It's on the top of the highest hill. You can't miss it."

What a hill! After several unsuccessful attempts to drive up it, even in low gear, everybody had to crawl out to lighten the load.

It was truly a beautiful place, with gardens and lawns expertly trimmed, and the house sitting grandly on the very peak of the hill. The African men who were about the place directed us to a grassy place among the trees to set up our tent.

Some time later an African dressed with more official flair drove in, introduced himself as the aide-de-camp, and invited us to stay in a small guesthouse behind the Governor's Lodge.

While we were exploring the possibilities of such a generous offer, we became a bit uneasy. Finally, we cautiously asked if he was sure the governor would not mind.

"I'll call and find out," he offered carelessly, and went to the lodge to phone.

While he was gone we decided among ourselves that the Dorsch family should accept the invitation, if it panned out. Allen and I were still excited about the adventure of sleeping out in the rough.

"You're wanted on the telephone, sir." The aide-de-camp had returned and was speaking to Victor.

Someone very politely chewed us out for camping there and wanted to know who had given us permission. Luckily, we had the backing of the police. That was all they said. Victor did not know to whom he had spoken, nor had the voice ordered us out.

"My sakes! Let's not stay in the house," Viola offered. "We can all stay in the tent tonight."

Shortly after midnight the police came to check on us, were satisfied, and soon left. The next morning we left very early, so as to avoid any direct encounter with His Honor, the Governor.

While Kampala is modern and beautiful, we had the feeling that we were kissing civilization good-bye when we came into the western section of Uganda.

The road into Fort Portal came to a dead end at a garage. There we asked about a camping site. Just as the fellow stepped out of the building to give us directions to the District Commissioner's office, the D.C. came pulling up in his car. We had an unusual welcome. He showed us where to camp under some pines, and gave us access to his private lavatory adjacent to his office.

The next day a lovely stretch of tarmac road ran us through a short section of the Ruwenzori, Mountains of the Moon, and then opened into wide prairies and grasslands. Some time later we entered Queen Elizabeth Park, passed through customs, entered Congo and the Prince Albert Park. Finally, we had entered our first real "storybook thrill" of jungle-creeping Africa. Topi, gazelle, impala, monkeys, elephants, buffalo—we saw them all throughout these two game parks.

Five glorious days we spent at Kisenyi on Lake Kivu. We pitched the tent a hundred feet from the water for the Dorsch family. Allen and I still preferred sleeping in the open. The sun filtered through the kapok and orange trees; the little lake waves lapped at the retaining wall. Nearby was a genuine miniature golf course and a refreshment stand that sold cokes.

There the weariness eased out of our bodies and spirits, and our eyes became more clear for the task of the year ahead. But one used to a routine of work cannot long endure an unscheduled maze of reading, sunning, swimming, writing letters, meditating, and sleeping, without soon becoming restless.

Goma, Rutshuru, Kisoro, Kabale. We had gone from the Congo to Uganda. It was evening when we arrived in Kabale, and we looked up the D.C.'s home for camping advice. He led us to the clump of buildings, the office of himself and others.

"Behind this building is a large lawn," he volunteered. "Perhaps you would wish to erect your tents there. You can drive around the back. There is water on tap where you can do a bit of washing up."

We thanked him, shook hands, and parted. We drove behind the building, parked the VW, and began to unload. Night was coming fast, and a light rain was falling.

"Let's just put our cots and sleeping bags here," someone suggested, motioning toward a veranda running along the full length of the building.

"Do you know what this building is?" Victor asked, a little surprised. "This is the district courthouse!"

"Wouldn't we feel stupid if someone would find us tomorrow morning, a bunch of dirty American missionaries, sleeping on the porch of the courthouse!"

The rain and the late hour were enough to eventually convince even those of us who were most doubtful about the propriety of the suggestion.

One year later I found myself again in the New York of East Africa—Nairobi. I was down in the African business section of the city arranging with an Indian for a bus trip.

It's not that I was wild about traveling on an African bus, but I was aiming to go far from the maddening cry of Euro-Asian-African cities and white farmlands. My destination was the little isolated village of Shirati on the Tanganyikan edge of Lake Victoria. The trip called for two days by bus. At the end of the first day I would be dropped off at a British hotel with a horrid European price tag on the pillow and tea for one night.

Arrangements had been made for me to go on a short safari with two of my old college friends, Maynard Kurtz and Donald Mellinger, also on short-term missionary teacher assignments. John Graybill, a mechanic, and his wife made up the rest of our little group.

It was the second day of our safari. The five of us had left the green hills and odd rocks of the country on the eastern shore of Lake Victoria and were now driving through the soft rolling grasslands of the Serengeti National Park.

Evening came in with us as we drove into the Seronera Camp, a lovely site nestled among acacia trees. High-peaked, grass-roofed huts marked a harmonious marriage of African architecture with European modernization—cement walls and floors, glass windows, refrigerators, and hot bath water.

"Man, where are the lions?" Mellinger-the-biologist, complained. "Let's see somethin' big for once!"

We had unloaded our camping equipment and had agreed to take a swing in the jeep through the outlying area south of campsite to spot some game. Since we could see nothing too exciting, Kurtz felt called upon to entertain us with wild animal incredibilities.

"See that tree—there?" He indicated with a finger. "A perfect place for a leopard to lie, crouched on that bottom limb. You know, if you're ever walking without a gun through the bush and see a leopard in a tree overhead, don't look at him; just keep walking. To stare at him will anger him. He'll spring immediately! But if you don't look him in the eye, you've broken the contact."

On the way back to camp, I remember mumbling something about how I would rather face death than to have it leap on my back.

"Think I'll bathe while supper is brewing," I said, and knelt to light a lantern. The African night had crept from the rolling plains to the campsite.

I crossed to the bathhouse, carrying high the lantern before me. Just as I stepped on the threshold, a black coil on the floor unraveled in the yellow pool of light and shot across fractions from my foot.

"There's a snake in my bath!" I yelled.

Mellinger-the-biologist came running—for his perfect specimen, no doubt. I held the light up for him to see. He took one look at the snake in the far corner, shrieked, "Black mamba," and fled. Since I didn't know a black mamba from a pink tango, Mellinger's alarm didn't register.

Graybill-the-mechanic, hearing the shriek, came running, armed with a long-handled brush. The snake had begun to climb the wall now. Mr. Mechanic crept in and clobbered its head against the wall while I held the light.

By this time Kurtz, Mellinger, and Mrs. Graybill had circled the bathhouse door and were awaiting the arrival of Graybill-Hero-Slayer, the crushed Mamba-Foe, and me.

On the way back to our sleeping huts, Mellinger quizzed, "Were you bitten?"

I had not thought of it. "Well," I said, "would've I known—if I were bitten?"

"Possibly. Quite possibly not. Their strike is so rapid that it's usually impossible to feel it penetrate."

"How long have I to live?"

"A half hour till your blood congeals."

I looked at my watch as I entered the door of the hut. Eight-twenty. A half hour yet. I remembered a bit of first-aid advice—"Keep still." Crawling slowly into bed, I began sorting through my mind for what should be done first. I decided on a letter to Mother. Between paragraphs of the letter, I instructed Mellinger and Kurtz on how to dispose of my possessions.

Thirty little minutes dragged by on heavy feet. Ten of

nine! I felt my pulse, jumped from the bed, and whirled through cartwheels around the room. I was yet alive!

"Maynard, will you go with me to the outhouse and hold the light?" I felt the need for a bit of support to venture into the night again.

He readily agreed and off we went. I had no more than sat down when I felt a flutter—a brush of something fuzzy. Snakes, I thought!

"Snakes!" I screamed, as I fled from the shanty.

Kurtz dropped the lantern to the ground and burst into laughter as I streaked past him. Unknown to me, a mamma bat and her two babies were trailing me.

"Stop it! Stupid!" I yelled angrily.

"Bats!" was all he could squeeze between laughs.

When dawn washed in over the east, none was so glad to be breaking camp as I.

I am never safe in describing the Serengeti Plains. I want to use all the trite, hackneyed expressions ever used —beautiful, vast, stupendous, awesome. But these really do not describe the feeling of wildness that ran along the seams of my naked emotions.

During the years in Somalia, I first became aware of a force operating upon me. I frequently had Walden experiences of isolation and nearly always practiced simplicity, particularly during my periods of isolation in the bush country or for mere hours of solitude on the wide, long beaches of the Indian Ocean. Something tore and cried within me for expression.

Somalia, a vast stretch of sand and bush country, filled me with the wild, alert feeling of being lost. But two other factors impressed me even more. One was the horizontal lines, and the other was the simplicity of components within the natural setting.

The horizontal lines of the broad level expanses of desert bush country and ocean caused me to stretch and stretch with my mind and eye. Sand, water, and sky—the elements of a beach-Walden; or grass, thorn trees, and sky —the elements of an inland setting, all spoke of simplicity.

Serengeti National Park in Tanganyika was the consummation of this gathering force. On a little knoll under some acacia trees, marked on the map as "Lion Hill," the eye saw only the sweep of the sky and the silent, naked curve of the earth. In that one glorious moment when my sense melted away, when my body became one great receptive pore, I felt that I had experienced in part what the romantic pantheists, the greatest of nature lovers, have tried to relate.

When I felt that I could absorb no more, the jeep rolled up to the edge of Ngorongoro Crater, 2,000 feet deep, twelve to fourteen miles across.

These are the kinds of places that haunt my memories. Sometimes I do not know if it was a dream I had of those lovely-sounding names—Serengeti, Ngorongoro, Kilimanjaro—that keeps coming back to be redreamed, or whether I had actually traversed those areas.

Ahead lay a road which was to lead us eventually to Mt. Kilimanjaro. The ascent of that 19,565 foot volcanic lump is a story in itself.

"It's the kind of mountain that probably lies only once in the path of a man's life," I remember philosophizing as we lay on our beds, stiff and sore. But now only the pleasantries of that five-day, seventy-mile hike remain. I keep imagining that I see another mountain looming on the horizon.

Chapter Nine

Margherita

"Ugh!" Driver Shirk moaned, "I feel a flat coming!"

"I smell one!" said a voice from the rear seat.

Indeed, it was just that. A flat tire. That wouldn't be so bad; one could always change to the spare, but this was the second one! Naturally, no one would have taken the time to fix the first flat two hours further back the road. But who would have thought the same joke could be played twice?

"Okay! Mammas, get out the Thermos for drinks. Babies, go to the toilet." With the last statement Shirk made a generous sweeping gesture in the general direction of the bush. "And we men will see about this dirty ol' flat."

At such time of mechanical crisis, I was never quite certain of my gender. I was not with the mission family long before I was known as an absolute idiot concerning even simple mechanical problems, though none were so cruel as to voice such a thought. So I was not sure that the cozy inclusiveness of the statement, "And we men will see about this dirty ol' flat," really included me. My small thoughts were interrupted with Shirk roaring again.

"Oh, brother! For a moment I forgot that this is our second flat and we have no spare! Have to waste time on the road fixin' old worn-out tires and tubes. You'd think this mission was poor or somethin'. Get out the repair kit from under the seat. Open the hood; take out a spark plug. Get ready to pump up. Bring the jack. Throw out the other flat tire." Everybody jumped into action, while Shirk ran about in frantic little circles.

Having done my share of the work—getting the repair kit from under the front seat—I sat back in the shade of a thorn tree to watch the other male occupants in this assembly-repair-line.

"*Nabadt.*" A Somali voice greeted me from behind.

"*Nabadt,*" I said, and turned to see two men and a small boy stepping from the edge of the bush to the middle of the road.

I was amazed again, as I always was, that here in this stretch of mile after mile of sand and thorn trees, Somali people seem to emerge from nowhere.

The two men, their skins tight, but a little gray with dust, stood poised, chewing small twigs, cleaning, and rubbing their brilliant teeth, and spitting frequently. The small boy glistened, his body taut with excitement. Occasionally they talked quietly among themselves.

"Americanos; are they not?"

"Indeed."

"The one leg of the machine is broken."

"But has it not three good ones yet? Cannot even an old camel go on three legs!" jabbered the small boy.

"Perhaps they wish to go quickly. The twelfth hour is near when the night comes."

"Ho! There is a strange thing! They have thrust the

tail of a snake into the heart of the machine."

Shirk was screwing the one end of the compressor hose into the spark plug opening. Someone inside the car was starting the engine. The hose rippled and sprang back slightly from where it had lain carelessly coiled in the soft dust. Spurts of air hissed from the opening and raised little puffs of dust.

"It is truly a snake!" The little boy screeched and dashed to the edge of the bush.

"*Kalei, kalei,* my little *yero*. It is no snake. It is only the breath from the heart of the machine."

"Yes, it is only air from the heart." The two men spat as if to show their disdain at such an ordinary thing.

The small boy returned to their side. To show that he was now brave he began to question, "But why do the Americanos put air in the round legs? Do not the legs of the donkey carts at the village Brava have sand in them?"

"Yes, little one, but they are old legs on those donkey carts. They are bad legs and the air has gone out of them, as when a camel kicks you in the stomach. When the air goes out quickly, it cracks."

"Ha! That is true, for even I have heard it."

"But how do the Americanos keep the air in the round legs of the machine?" The small boy again.

"*Shupta!* Must you ask so many questions? Perhaps I will not know all the answers."

"But. . . ." The small boy was cut off.

"Be quiet! If you ask so many questions perhaps the snake will give you chase."

"I have no fear. It is not a snake. It is only air, as you yourself have said. It is only air that they are putting in the round leg, such as when I blow into a small piece of a camel's intestine and it becomes big and round." The small boy quivered at the true words he had just spoken, not knowing that he was going to say them. He quivered at his own discovery.

Basking in that triumph, he attacked another. "I know how the air stays in the round legs of the Americanos' machine."

"Indeed?"

"A jinni squeezes it shut!" He was overcome with giggles.

"My little *yero,* sometimes you are so stupid that I think only a hyena could have given birth to you."

Both men chuckled; the small boy giggled again.

"Ho! And there is another strange thing. The one leg is put on the machine. Fine. But the other is thrown into the back. Now that is strange. It has five legs!"

Driver Shirk had dropped the spare tire into the back of the old Chevy. Children were quarreling for seats at the windows. Mammas, already seated, were fanning themselves, the inside of the car being an inferno from sitting in the direct sunlight.

I rose from my seat under the thornbush, dusted my trousers, "Salaamed" the Somali men, and shuffled toward the car. Another two hours of sun, sand, and thorns lay ahead.

They told me that Africa was slow and I answered: yes, it was true, and yet I had seen time go by on little scurrying feet. Nine months were gone since I had arrived in Mogadiscio. Where had they gone? I didn't know. Only the calendar verified it. Sometimes I wondered if my days still had twenty-four hours. Seeing the need and knowing why we were there and then observing the little response, I prayed God to work more quickly through my life and the lives of His missionaries His plan for these people.

It was Ramadan, the Muslim month of fasting. Since

the night school in Mogadiscio was closed, I asked Director Keener for permission to go and join Allen Brubaker for the month. He was the only Pax fellow at Torda, a village south of Margherita. The others were on a visit to Ethiopia.

"Perhaps I can help hoe his bean rows, or whatever it is that they have planted," I offered.

"Well. . . ." Uncle Clayton was thinking.

"Or drive their ox," I continued.

"I have a better idea," began Uncle. "Now that we have the land for the mission station at Margherita, Shirk is already working like mad at the building program. Even though he had ten or more Somalis on the construction crew, I believe he could find something for you to do."

So I was transferred to the Margherita station, 265 miles south of Mogadiscio, to help in the building program.

I am not sure if Roy Shirk, the mission builder, knew who was being shoved off on him or not. But at the end of the first day he had a small idea of my potential.

A half-dozen metals barrels had been gathered in which to store water. Roy wanted the tops cut out of them.

"Here's a cold chisel and a hammer. Just cut around the top, following the outer edge," Roy instructed and then turned to his own work.

By the end of the morning, halfway through the job, my lily-white teacher's hands were two great inflated scarlet blisters!

The job that consumed most of my time was experimenting with a concrete-block-making-machine. I don't think I had ever seen a block machine in the States—for certain I had never operated one. It was an impressive piece of machinery, and reminded me of the pictures I had seen of Gutenberg's press. But it wasn't all quite so simple as it may sound. It took considerable time experimenting before good, square, solid blocks could be produced.

"We are here to work ourselves out of a job," Shirk said. "The sooner we can help these African people to do things for themselves, the better."

And that was exactly what happened. The first week I ran the machine myself; that is, I pushed and pulled levers and tramped pedals. I kept four men working: two men hand-mixed the ingredients, one filled the chamber, and another carried the pressed blocks away. Then I turned it over to the Somali men. They did quite well and continued on alone for months and months of block-making.

In spite of such assembly-line procedures, our daily output was quite minimal. It was Ramadan. The men only worked five hours a day, from six to eleven in the morning. I usually came on the job at seven. The most we turned out in a five-hour period were 150 blocks. But I felt certain that in several weeks the Somali men would surpass that figure considerably, perhaps phenomenally.

The first small rain had whispered through the dry countryside a few weeks earlier, marking the end of a nine-month dry season. Now rains tore down daily, and would continue for the next several months, unmercifully slashing at the earth.

The rains meant spring for us. The desert broke out in blossom. The thorn trees were sprinkled with small flowers, lavender, pink, and peach. Already a fringe of green, misty mint and olive, brushed the tips of the thorns. A fuzz of grass sprang up on the desolate sweeps of barren plains.

It was again another Ramadan season and again I was spending it with the Margherita folks. We were spinning along a small road heading for some Bantu village along the Juba River. It was Friday; Victor and Viola Dorsch were on their weekly visit to preach the Word and instruct catechumens.

We visited two villages in the morning, slowly ate a packed lunch under some mango trees along an irrigation canal, and then stretched out in the shade for a "siesta," talking to each other in low, lazy voices. It was the time of day when the landscape quivered; heat waves blurred the view and played tricks with the eyes.

When the late afternoon coolness eased in, we drove off to yet another village. Usually we gathered in the courtyard of some Christian's home. One of the Christians would read the Scriptures and pray. We would give the handle of the portable phonograph a few last turns and listen to some discussion of a Bible story or parable. All this was before Victor had studied Swahili and could preach in that language. Then we would all join in loudly singing hymns. Although I could not understand a word of the Swahili, I joined in singing, for it was an easy enough language to pronounce, or at least to slur over when singing.

Sitting on a mat and singing *"Tazama, Uishi,"* I remembered a Christmas I had spent with the Margherita missionaries at Mofi, a small river village six miles north of Margherita.

A goat and maybe a sheep cooked over an open fire in the courtyard. In the hut the group of Somali Christians and we missionaries sang the Christmas story. Soon huge bowls of steaming rice were carried in to be eaten with the meat.

One of my last visits to Margherita was about nine months before going home to the States. It was the occasion of our annual mission conference. Three African pastors and a missionary from the Tanganyika Mennonite Church had come to aid us in our exploratory work among the Bantu tribes living along the Juba River. Now the team was bringing us inspirational messages.

The pressure lamp hissed as the African brother spoke, his voice barely above a conversational level, his long fingers touching the air with sparse gestures. What is it? I asked myself that evening in the classroom during the closing session. What is it that they have which is almost uncanny?

It was not the delivery, for that was nearly artless. And the words were simple, sometimes too obvious. But the message—as long as one trusts in his own capacities, wit, and training (thus expressing that God is hardly needed to aid in His own work), God seems to let a person remain on that level, until he discovers that even as a Christian he must relinquish his hopes of being a success and doing a good piece of mission work on his own steam. For the Lord would have His people grow weaker and weaker, so that He might grow stronger and stronger, only that.

Was it not the same truth I had learned during my stay at Mahaddei, when in desperation I had finally turned to the Lord and said, "I have no other missionary, no other Christian, not even a wife to whom I may now turn for advice and encouragement. And as you have known all along, and as I have just begun to learn, all my resources are soon exhausted and still the problems come. This work's yours. I'm no longer going to try to do anything. I'm just going to let my soul sit down and have a big rest in you." Had I foolishly mistaken the truth of that discovery as being applicable for only that one lesson? Now I was hearing it again, and I found the Spirit in me saying, "Amen."

The highlight of the conference was the receiving of the five African believers into our church fellowship, and then having communion, and sharing in our humble, Mennonite tradition of a footwashing service.

Chapter Ten

Thorns

Were I a great slab of weather-beaten outdoorsman, my big-game hunting record would be a mean thorn in my pride. The biggest animal, but most stupidly shot, was a hippo. About the rest, little needs to be said. Somalia will not miss the four gazelle, a few baboon, a pig, and some dik-dik which I eventually hit.

Hunting was a thorn in my spirit, for I discovered I was to be denied the thrill I had observed other men wallowing in when their bullet went home, or better, when they were retelling the event in the dim camp light of an African night.

Hunting was a thorn because I found that I was being pressured into conforming with the traditions of the sport. The blood and guts, the slit throat, the blood squirting from the bullet puncture, staining the sleek coat, the light dying in the eyes of a wild thing—all this I was supposed to enjoy. To like it was somehow to attest to my manliness.

I had loaded myself down with a Winchester 30-06 because I had been told that it was the thing to take. The animals hadn't a chance. We could chase them in the LandRover across the open plains, quickly alight, and fire at their fleeing white-flanked backsides.

The Somali bush is not the lovely flat-top-acacia-treed plains that one sees in Kenya and Tanganyika. The dry flats of Somalia produced scrubby trees and spreading tight clumps of thornbushes. There, on the long hot walks after my gazelle, thorns reached out and tore at my clothes, distracting my quiet thoughts.

One afternoon when I was visiting the Pax men at Torda, Allen Brubaker had to drive a man to the river to cross the ferry. At his urging I took my rifle along.

"On the way back from the river, it will be evening and we'll see if any deer will be out feeding on the open plains," Allen said as we drove along, keeping our eyes peeled for a form of any gazelle that might be resting in the shade during this hottest part of the day.

"The early morning and again an hour before sunset when it is cool are the best times to see game," Allen continued. "They're up on the move to graze or water. During the hot hours they take to the bush and it's almost impossible to hunt for them there."

Lying across the fender of the LandRover a few hours later, steadying the rifle on the spare tire mounted on the hood, I took shots at some gazelle grazing at the foot of low red hills. They were barely discernible, yet the low sun threw its long rays under the trees and highlighted their white markings perceptibly. I was amazed at the distance my shots were covering.

"How far is it over there," I called out to Allen.

"Nearly a half mile," he noted. "But you seem to be shooting a little low."

It was my first experience with the rifle. I had never

hunted in the States, and living in Mogadiscio did not offer any chance of using the gun. So I was quite new about it. But mostly I was surprised at the distance my rifle could shoot. Not that it was an unusual gun; I was just unfamiliar with its range.

And this was skill? I remember thinking the beasts wouldn't have a chance when I boned up on the knowledge of my weapon. But I proved wrong, for they still had many a chance. I was always waiting too long to fire, or aiming too low.

Perhaps my whole hunting life got off to a wrong start. Sixteen hours after my plane landed in Mogadiscio, I was thumping along on the back of a pickup truck headed for "some big stuff." The night had been spent on a canvas cot, the wooden frame carving into my shoulder blades. The night before that had been spent on the airplane, curled up like a question mark. Now we were heading for the bush for big game. We five missionary men and one Somali had two guns among us.

This was to be an exploration for happier hunting grounds. The Somali herdsmen who walked into Mahaddei to swap gossip and drink tea had been telling of great herds of oryx roaming a plain northwest of the village.

We had arisen in the early dark and thundered along over an old railroad bed, the tracks having been removed by the British during their occupation. Now we dodged along camel trails, and then the sun was hot upon us. Still we drove furiously, and still there was nothing but a few dik-dik and guinea fowl.

We limped back to the compound that evening, battered, irritated, and completely empty-handed. I felt sorry for the mission folks, for they were very tired of eating camel and goat meat. The only relief in the whole day was that there would be no processing of meat late into the night.

We were on the little road that ran south from Torda. There where the last of the red sandy hills fall away to the wide plains rolling down to the river, a few of us men were driving along in the LandRover on a little hunt. We were heading for the jungle-like swampland along the river where the vegetation was thick and where we thought at least some water buck could be found even during this driest season.

After walking in pairs for hours, we were about to give it up as a bad hunt. Suddenly, round the corner of the little path, we came upon two Somali men who with a bow and arrow had just shot a lioness. They were now skinning it.

"Are there lions in this area?" Roy Shirk asked the men, hardly believing his eyes.

"Indeed. Here is one." They motioned toward the skinned cat.

"It's sure news to me," Roy replied, shaking his head.

"Well, brethren, if that is the case, I think I'll head back to the LandRover," Uncle Clayton said. He had been walking around for hours in that lion-infested area with only a shotgun, hoping to shoot guinea fowl.

"I can hardly believe they could kill a lion with an arrow," I commented.

"They use poisoned arrows," Roy informed me.

He talked for a little while in Somali with the men. Finally, he announced that he had just succeeded in purchasing the lioness' skin for five American dollars.

"The men said there are about fifteen or twenty more lions in this area," he added, draping the skin over sticks to carry back to the vehicle.

When we returned to the LandRover, Uncle Clayton was chuckling nervously. "You know what? When I got back to the car and was going to unload the shotgun, I discovered that I didn't even have a shell left in it. It makes me weak when I think of how I was walking around in that lion country with an empty shotgun. Brother!"

One afternoon during Ramadan season I went with Allen down to the riverside to cut the tall grass that grew there. This we loaded on the LandRover truck to haul back to feed to his oxen. It was on the return trip and the evening coolness was slipping in over the hot plains. We had put our guns behind the seat, "just in case." Now we had them out and were scanning the scene ahead.

"Since you're in the city so much, I'll be kind and let you shoot at everything we see on this trip." Allen laughed and added, "Furthermore, I think my license is about filled up for this year. Today's your last chance on this license for the year, and before you head back to the city for teaching."

We had not driven far when we both spied a gerenuk standing on a little rise on the left side of the road, browsing among some bushes.

Allen immediately braked and followed with instructions. "This is real good! You can ease out your side. Don't throw the door open too wide. Slip up along the side of the fender and lay across the hood. Prop your gun on the hood and take plenty of time to aim. He hasn't seen or caught wind of us yet."

I followed his instructions almost instinctively. I remembered to aim just a bit higher, since I had been shooting too low at other times. I released the safety catch, paused a moment to control my breathing, peered through the sights again and fired. The "punk" of the bullet hitting

116

the target followed on the tail of the gun's explosion.

The gerenuk stood, shocked for a moment, and then slowly eased into the grass, slumping forward on its long, almost giraffe-like neck. Its long, thin legs thrashed for a few seconds. Then a great stillness settled over the form.

"Bravo! It's yours!" Allen was out of the car, whipping a knife from a sheath. "Here, quick slit the throat."

I had paused only a few feet in front of the car, pleasingly surprised, yet lost, like a man who had suddenly forgotten something. Allen's cries brought me back quickly. We ran together, he handing me his knife.

There lay the graceful golden chestnut body with sandy brown flanks, and sparkling white underparts. Now down over the sleek coat a stream of dark red blood flowed. Squirts of blood jerked out from the gaping hole in the chest. The great black eyes were open, the gleam fast dying to a dull glaze.

I lifted the head gingerly by the lyre-shaped horn, tilting it back to taut the neck, making it easier to cut.

The golden mystery of life flowed out of its body and with it my golden feeling of pleasure. Death crept in and again I was lost, like a man suddenly remembering something. I weakly handed the knife to Allen, who proceeded with cutting the throat. To this day, I don't believe Allen has ever told anyone of my weak spirit.

We drove the rest of the way home to Torda in silence.

"It was the first lovely thing you ever killed, wasn't it?" he asked.

"Yes."

"It's a strange thing. And it affects people differently."

A year later, and again during the Ramadan season, I joined the Margherita folks on a hunting trip. We loaded up the Chevy truck: a. barrel of water, lots of foodstuffs, several cans of gasoline, and sleeping bags. We drove for two hours to a place in the bush west of Margherita called Afmadu. Here we picked up a police escort, who acted as a guide, and proceeded to the interior of Somalia.

It is a good thing to have a Somali escort along on such trips through new territory and over almost pathless plains and through unmarked bush. This I found to be true from experience. One thinks that he will remember where he has come by, forcing himself to make conscious notes of a certain tree formation or arrangement. Yet if he walks for a few minutes, turns a few corners and then heads back, the view seems new. I marveled at the strange sense with which the Somalis guided one through the bush.

We came upon a herd of giraffes. A few of us clamored to be let down from the truck long enough to try to get some photographs of them. I think I would still be out in the bush photographing giraffes had it not been for the impatience of the hunters who remained in the truck. They began to blow the horn. They never knew it, but I was not taking pictures all that time, for I was gone much longer than I had promised. I simply could not find my way to the truck, and I had gone only a few hundred yards. The bush had closed in around me and everywhere the landscape was new and looked the same. But the honking of the truck horn helped me to find my direction.

The five of us missionaries and two Somalis hunted all morning. The Somalis were along to cut the throats and say a few Islamic words during the act, thus making the meat edible for themselves and other bushmen to whom we later gave some of our kill.

That night we built a great fire and roasted gazelle steaks, curled up in our sleeping bags on the ground by the side of the truck, and dreamed of lions.

The next morning we hunted from sunup till noon. I

got two Grant's gazelle and one gerenuk. The others got considerably more. When we returned to Afmadu to let off the police escort, we gave much of the meat to various Somalis. They were most grateful for the meat, for it was hard work for them to track down deer for food.

The Roy Shirks were leaving Margherita to return to the States. Dave Miller, who had come to continue the building, planned to give an open-fire roast for the Somali workmen in honor of the Shirks. This was several days after our Afmadu trip. Now we needed fresh meat.

We decided to go out late in the evening and sleep out and be there early in the morning to hunt. We drove well into the bush country below Torda, and decided that this would be a good place to stop and sleep. We lay in our sleeping bags, praying, swapping gossip, pondering the stars, and speculating about America.

Suddenly a lion grunted. We all jumped to our feet and listened. We decided it was far enough away, so we lay down again. The deep, deep grunts and the long purrs continued. I thought they kept getting nearer. Suddenly, I jumped up and ran for the truck, trailing my sleeping bag behind me. When I got there, Roy, Allen, and Dave were following me. They all confessed that they didn't like lying out there, but they didn't want to be "chicken" and be the first to run for cover! Allen and I slept on the back of the truck, Dave in the cab, and Roy on the roof.

The next morning while we were hunting, we sat on the top of the truck and looked down into the thornbush. A short distance away tall grass moved and out trotted a brown and yellow, shaggy male lion. When we headed the truck in his direction, he drifted off in the tall dry grass. Only a slight ripple in the grass could be seen, and then stillness folded back over the savannah and thornbush.

Chapter Eleven

Sketches

September, 1957

I was never in a Muslim mosque, nor have I knelt toward Mecca and listened to a Muslim pray, and I can't even quote passages from the Koran, but maybe I'll have to. Maybe I'll have to identify myself with the people in this way to understand them. Maybe I must be "made all things to all men, that I might by all means save some [one]."

My personal commitment, or as I like to think of it— my conspiracy with God, began a year and a half ago. In the back of my journal I had scribbled these words: "My commitment to God—to go anywhere, to do anything, at any time, with anyone, or no one." These words didn't come just after an overnight emotional upheaval. It took the Lord almost eight weeks to get this out of me. Sure, I was a Christian, and a good Mennonite, too. But that wasn't enough, because my ears heard a word behind me saying, "This is the way, walk ye in it, when ye turn to the right hand, and when ye turn to the left. . . .

"And, behold, I am with thee, and will keep thee in all places whither thou goest, and will bring thee again into this land; for I will not leave thee, until I have done that which I have spoken to thee of."

October, 1957

I am all tied up with teaching and attempting to learn a new language. After these first days of classes I am as hoarse as a mule! I think my one lung has collapsed; but upon a more thorough anatomical analysis, I believe my nerves did it all—all to them I owe. Somehow the Lord always gets me through these first days of teaching.

I am finding that water has the same hypnotic effect on me as fire. Here we live two hundred yards from the Indian Ocean. I can sit and watch it by the hour. And the moon on it is indescribable! At night I go up on the housetop and look about—but particularly to see the moon reflected on the ocean. If I were the melancholy, romantic type of person, this could be fatal!

November, 1957

Reading *Time* is a thrilling event living on this side of the Atlantic and so close to the Middle East countries, this touchy spot of the world. I do wonder what Somalia will be like in 1960 when she gets her independence. Many people think she is not nearly ready for it. If she isn't ready, I'd like to place the blame right at Italy's door. The sub-efficiency in all matters of life (except wine drinking and death) is astonishing and could be dated with the Ottoman Turks. But the most impossible thing for my students to grasp is that Somalia is not an important country in the world.

I told them perhaps only one American in a hundred could tell me where Somalia is located, what countries lie next to it, and who is administering it. They thought I was nothing but a propagandist attempting to intimidate them.

December, 1957

I think if people at home could only know how human all these folks called "foreign missionaries" are, it would once and forever explode all the glorified ideas of mission work and workers. Why can't people be more realistic! But I've just been told that my realism tends to border on pessimism.

Whatever led me to believe that coming here would solve or dissolve the problems of life—of my life! I can never tell. Having opened this one door, I find I am in a hall with six other doors, each leading somewhere other than to dead closets. And who can know the doors beyond these doors? My conspiracy with God is sometimes frightening; yet I thank Him for the opportunity of choice.

January, 1958

It would be so good to chitchat again with some of my old college buddies about life, the church, Christian philosophy, and practice. I don't know where I stand. I keep changing—fluctuating would be a better analysis, I guess. One day I am a liberal and the next a conservative. And then one day I'm both.

I have the silly fear that I am maturing too fast! After all, I'm living with a grandpa and grandma day in and day out. Not that I don't love them. I don't know of a more pleasing old couple to live and work with. I guess it is just the young social contact I miss. There are some younger missionaries out here to talk and argue with, but I am not sure that they are any better off than I, for they are just as isolated.

February, 1958

It seems to me that these Muslims do not have to worry

with an interpretation of life. Their religion is so almost fatalistic. Whenever anything happens, they brush over it easily by saying, "God wills it." Thus evil, tragedy, and sorrow commonly come and go. Sometimes life seems cheap.

But Christians are left with the burden of pounding on heaven and pleading for a revelation of life. The amazing thing is that when we derive the answer it stands as a startling paradox to the burden of inquiry. The sweep of fresh peace and surge of strange strength saturates life with new meaning.

March, 1958

I was just reading journals I kept during college days. Horrors! I suppose every college person goes through a crisis period sometime within the last two years of his college days. For myself I definitely know that "bog-down" came during the latter part of my junior year. I am discovering this to be more and more true the further I move on this side of those years. For eight weeks I did not go to church or prayer circles; neither did I read my Bible or pray. But I have reasons to believe that this was more common with some of my college buddies than was the exception.

I had brought all my journals with me to Somalia. The other night I was nosing through some of the muck and came across some arresting entries. I was rather disturbed. The person revealed and the life lived was so different from my present. I burned much of what was in them and am still in the process of screening them.

April, 1959

Impractical Christianity—now there's a thing! I think of two kinds of impractical Christians. The first is a person who lives a pious, conservative, busy life without

Christian service. The other kind of impractical Christian is the person who lives on the outer margin of Christianity —so close to the world, that the lines and patterns become blurred. The day I discovered I had lost my impractical Christianity, I think I was well on the good way to recovery.

May, 1959

The beach is empty and I have come alone for an evening walk. My motor scooter lies on its side against a sand dune a short ways back. I have headed north, as I always do; it's the direction one should go, for behind him lies the city.

I find that line on the shore where the waves have run up the beach, packing, washing, leveling the sand. To my right the ocean heaves, and has started another dark wave up the long shore. It levels as it comes toward me, running fast now and frothy. To my left hieroglyphic scrawls, tracks, mounts, and holes in the loose sand record an afternoon's transactions. The evening breeze puffs spurts of sand stinging against my bare legs.

My slow pace alerts the silly crabs which run sideways in a frenzied retreat, drowning themselves in an undertow. The last bright evening light catches the gleaming breast of a sea gull wheeling alone out over the ocean. And I feel within me the rush of wings which would lift me and send my spirit soaring higher than I have known, but a fear of the higher places slows the upward lift of that call.

"Take me up slowly on ascending wings," I say, "for the cold ocean still heaves below."

"But there is light up here," the wings of the gull seem to flash back.

June, 1959

Five o'clock! For me this is the time of day when it is

so hard to concentrate. It is the time I want, somehow, always to pray. Knowing surely that the heat of the day has passed safely, and feeling within me the relieving promises of night—well, somehow I always feel that this is my hour when love and life begin to flow back through me.

July, 1959

The other night three Somali students ate dinner with us. This was their first experience of eating with Europeans, as they call us. They were courageous fellows, attempting the various American dishes more vigorously than we missionaries do when offered their native cooking. It was interesting to observe that the gesture of sharing a meal together helped to dissolve certain barriers. We engaged in one of the most free exchange of ideas since I have known them.

August, 1959

I have just been thinking about heaven! It seems that most of us expect to find in heaven (among other blessings) those things that we have been denied while living on the earth. Or vice versa, to *not* find in heaven what we have had to endure on earth. This is probably true in other world religions. In the Koran I have been reading about the Muslim's idea of paradise.

"And besides these there shall be two other gardens of a dark green. In each of them shall be two fountains pouring forth plenty of water. In each of them shall be fruits, and palm trees, and pomegranates. Therein shall they delight themselves, lying on green cushions and beautiful carpets."

September, 1959

"No more sea." What strange words I ran across recently in Revelation. I picture John as sitting in the soft sand gazing out over the hot, glimmering sea. Above him a tall, thin palm waves its green branches in the morning sunlight. Then comes the cool, comforting promise of the Spirit's whispers that there will be "no more sea." It was this sea that was separating him from his home and friends.

But the symbol doesn't make sense here in Somalia. Here it is hot, dry, barren. Water is wealth—a premium. So this promise of a heaven without a sea may not be cherished by my Somali friends. Possibly the "pure river of water of life" in the twenty-second chapter of Revelation will suffice!

October, 1959

Recently there has been much excitement in the school. The American government promised to send fourteen young men to the States to study for one year. The Somali government gave a series of tests to determine who should go. Of the fourteen selected, six are from our school. This makes us quite happy to know that our work is accepted. Really, there is little hatred of foreigners here in Somalia, but it does not mean that they are sympathetic enough to accept the Gospel.

November, 1959

My Somali students have no idea at all how big the world is. Some of them asked me if my parents are never going to come and see me. The most ridiculous thing was when they asked if America is further away than Chisimaio —a town about 275 miles south of Mogadiscio! Some of them have heard of two other places in America—Washington and New York. Everybody thinks America is all skyscrapers and millionaires. And since we are Americans, they think we must be rich too. We can't convince them otherwise though we do live cheaply here.

December, 1959

The Somali greet each other with the word, *nabadt* (peace). Ironically, one of the pressing issues, it seems to me, for the new statesmen is to calm the squabblings and weld the multi-factious tribal feelings into a national spirit. That is, to transform the casual, everyday greeting of peace *(Nabadt, nabadt)* into a vital internal and foreign policy of *nabadt*.

January, 1960

"To be put in trust with the Gospel" (I Thess. 2:4)— now there's some words that slap-bang me in the eye this morning. I (but why?) have been put in trust of the Gospel? And how I dillydally around! I'm afraid I don't know much of the "power of the Gospel" in my life. And the next phrase of Scripture—"even so we speak." Those are Paul's words—not mine! I'm too slow, too civilized to speak the Gospel! Oh, I can say a nice mouthful at the proper place and time. It's so easy to "speak of the Gospel" in churches and prayer meetings. But Paul spoke the Gospel wherever he found a man with ears to hear. Lord, I want some of that. But help me to speak the truth of the Gospel always in love. Help me to watch that edge in my voice when I do speak of Gospel-things.

February, 1960

I am learning to see the fine, subtle beauty in a desert. When I am exposed to the silent, naked sweep of the wide expanses of bush and sky, there's something inside that gets all tied up like an acute attack of cramps. Something wild inside goes out to meet and commune with the wild of nature.

March, 1960

Now that I have been through the mill of mission life a bit, I feel sort of like giving it up. At least I've got to get home and sit in the quiet someplace and think it all over—this business of missions in our century. But I know that will happen, once this is in my blood and spirit—I'll probably be crazy enough to say "Yes" and come back out later. But I'm not coming out again without further education, a wife, and some money!

April, 1960

When Somalia gains her independence she will be rudely awakened to the obvious truth that it wrought no magic or tricks. When she is free from Mamma-Italy and Papa-U.N., I think she will probably discover some bad boys in her own backyard attempting to lure her. She will have to work hard and bitterly to keep peace within her own Islamic Somali family.

May, 1960

When Hershey Leaman told me that he found it more difficult (emotionally) to leave Tanganyika and return home than it was for him to leave the States to come out to East Africa, I thought that he was hard. But I know what he means. I cried behind my sunglasses the whole way down the runway, until the plane lifted off and headed for home.

Chapter Twelve

Incense

One of my Somali students had come to my house in the morning to invite me to his wedding.

"But Abdulcadir, I didn't know that you had a girl friend, or were engaged, or that you even wanted a wife."

"I didn't know it either, Mr. Eby."

"What do you mean? What didn't you know?"

"I didn't know until a month ago that I was being given a wife, that I would have to marry her."

"My, this is fast work."

"Indeed!"

"But you do like her?"

"How do I know!"

"How do you know? Well. . . ."

"How do I know if I like her? I have never met her. In fact, I do not remember having ever seen her!"

"Wait, this is too much!"

"For me, too!"

"I do not know what to think. It is so very different. You say that you have never met her?"

"Mother says that when I was a small boy I used to play with her and her brothers and sisters. But when she became about twelve she went into . . . what do you call it in English? . . . confinement? . . . you know, wears a veil over her face all the time and only seldom comes out of the house."

"But haven't you seen her this month, now that you know you are going to marry her?"

"Only one time! She was going along the street and some friends pointed her out to me. But she had her face completely covered. So can I not say that I have truly never seen her? For what are clothes but only a cover?"

"Do you want to get married?" I finally asked, for I had detected from his manner that he did not seem to anticipate the occasion.

"No, I don't want to get married!" he barked back. "I am about eighteen; I have two years of secondary school to finish. Then I hope to get a scholarship to study in Italy, or perhaps just in Kenya, if my English improves. But a wife! How can I do this with a wife? Oh, Mr. Eby, you are lucky to have no wife yet!"

"Indeed?"

"Indeed! For look, you have gotten an education; you have traveled and seen some of the world. . . ."

"But when I go home, I am going to get a wife!"

"Ah, that will be a good time to get one."

There was a lull in the conversation as we both sat thinking of our future wives, he in mild agony, I with wistful anticipation.

"But you will come to my wedding?" he asked, rising to go.

"I certainly will, Abdulcadir."

130

It was Thursday, the day for Abdulcadir's wedding. I dressed as handsomely as I could, for I supposed that it would be a gala performance, knowing that Abdulcadir came from a rich family.

The wedding was scheduled to begin at four o'clock. It was three-thirty. I was crossing the town on my old motor scooter. Sherif Ahmed Abbas, a cousin to Abdulcadir, was riding on the seat behind me. He had come to supply me directions to the place of the wedding, and would be translating the ceremony for me.

We arrived near the place, parked the scooter, and walked the last few blocks. The narrow, one-way street in front of the large Credito Somalo building was closed.

Opposite the Credito was a three-story apartment built in the shape of an "L." The short angle of the "L" came out to the edge of the street. There was no sidewalk. The end of the building and the narrow street met with nothing between. Adjacent to the other arm of the "L" an outdoor teashop scattered tables and chairs over a crumbling cemented plaza, which extended to the L-shaped apartments.

Now a high wire had been stretched from the corner of the teashop, across the narrow street to a hook on the wall of the Somalo Credito building. Large sheets of bright orange and blue cloth interspersed with huge squares of Oriental rugs hung from the wire. The two wings of the old stone apartment and the canvas rug divider formed a large courtyard.

"We'll sit there." Sherif motioned toward the other side. We stepped inside and crawled carefully past other seated guests toward some empty chairs.

In the middle of this courtyard a small platform had been erected.

"They're just some tables pushed together and covered

with those rugs," Sherif commented.

The rugs covering the tables were smaller than the ones hanging along the walls, but they were more intensely colored. Chairs faced the platform from two sides, so that half the guests faced the other half. Small potted palm trees were scattered around the edges of the courtyard and around the platform.

On the rugs which covered the platform were six large brilliant cushions. A microphone was the only other prop in the setting.

Sherif and I had no sooner sat down than it began to rain. Luckily we were near an opening. We dashed to cover on one of the porches of a nearby building. Behind us other guests were taking refuge in the apartment doorways, the teashop, and the porch of the Credito building. A few guests apparently decided to sit it out, for they didn't stir the least. Some hoisted umbrellas, which they had carried with them.

The rain was a light one, lasting only fifteen minutes. Soon the sun burned; steam rose from the macadam street, and the wedding guests wandered back to their chairs. It was cool in the courtyard, for the buildings threw long shadows from the late afternoon sun.

From the moment I entered the courtyard and looked over the guests I thought something was strange, but I could not immediately spot the oddity. The guests were an assorted group. Some old men, with white cloths wrapped lightly about their heads, fingered their prayer beads. Many of the men, even the younger ones, wore the typical Somali skirt. But they were new or at least clean ones, very long and bright with green and red bars, or more sober blues. Some of the men wore the short-sleeved khaki suit, adapted from Italian styles. Here and there a few of the younger men were dressed completely in a

132

European manner, as was Sherif, who wore a white shirt with black bow tie, a navy blue suit, black shoes and socks. Suddenly the thing that was strange struck me. They were all men! There was not a woman among the guests.

"Where are the women?" I asked Sherif.

"In the house there." He gestured with his lower lip toward the apartment.

"Don't women ever come to Muslim weddings?"

"Not ours. And not even the bride. Our tribe is very orthodox in its religious practices. The women are there behind the closed shutters. They can see all that will go on through the little slits in the shutters. You will hear them, too!"

Three young men came out from behind a cloth screen, slipped off their shoes, and stepped up on to the platform. One carried with him a piano accordion, its plastic shell taped together at several places; a few keys were missing. Another fellow carried a guitar. The third fellow, carrying no instrument, stepped to the microphone. The other two circled about him.

"There's Hassan! I didn't know that he sang for entertainment."

"They are not going to entertain. They are singing passages from the Koran."

It was a strange union of East and West. Their instruments were European, but their songs were wailing, minor, Arabic chants. The effect was slightly torturous and seemed to go on much longer than was really necessary. But then I can well imagine that Handel's "Hallelujah Chorus" would strike my Somali friends as a ridiculous piece of fancy monotony.

A mullah, heavy with age and the dignity of his office, shuffled toward the platform. He paused long enough to slip out of his shoes and then mounted the steps leading to the platform. Once there, he settled slowly onto one of the large yellow cushions, crossed his legs under him, and adjusted his robes. Under one arm he carried a large Koran.

The wedding "wail" having ended, the musical trio stepped from the platform, taking the microphone with them.

A hush crept over the guests and they looked up expectantly. Now from behind the cloth screen a figure stepped out and moved toward the platform.

"But who is that?" I whispered to Sherif.

"That's Gelani. He is the oldest and so will be the first to be married."

"The first! How many are getting married?"

"Five."

"Five? But I thought it was just Abdulcadir who was getting married?"

"Oh, no! Abdulcadir, and his brother, one of his half brothers, who is a son from one of his father's other wives, and two of his cousins."

"But do you never just have a wedding for one man?"

"Sometimes. But we like this better. With only one man you cannot have a very big *fiesta*. But with five getting married you can have a *fiesta grande!*"

The first man, whom Sherif called Gelani, had climbed to the platform and was now sitting on one of the cushions, with his legs tucked under him. He faced the mullah.

"What are they saying?" I asked Sherif, for they were speaking softly to each other in Arabic.

"Oh, they're saying something like this:

"The mullah will say, 'What is your name?'

"The groom will give his name.

"The mullah: 'Is it indeed true that you wish to be married?'

134

"The groom is answering affirmatively.

"The mullah: 'Who is it that you wish to marry?'

"Then the groom gives the name of the girl to whom he is betrothed.

"The mullah then chants some verses from the Koran."

The air was split with a piercing joy cry, a shrill noise made with the tongue moving rapidly back and forth in the mouth and throwing the voice into a high register. The microphone had been transferred to the women behind the shutters. As soon as the groom had started to name his bride, the women drowned out the rest of the ceremony with their cries.

The groom stepped from the platform. He was dressed in a European suit and tie. Over this was thrown a long flowing beige cloak, beautifully embroidered. A white cloth for the head, fastened by bars forming a square crown, dropped down the groom's back. He carried a long scimitar, stunningly overlaid with silver and ivory.

The actual ceremony was short, much shorter than our Christian marriage ceremony. They had something of the same vows as we had, promising to protect and care for their wives. However, they did not have to promise to live with them till death do part them. But even in Somalia the ease with which a Muslim could traditionally divorce his wife was changing. Times were when they could repeat three times, "I divorce thee," and that was the end of a marriage contract. But today Islamic laws are being modified after the pattern of European civil laws.

And so they got married, the five of them. The oldest first and the youngest last, who appeared to be no more than seventeen.

"But Sherif, why did their fathers make them get married if they really didn't want to?"

135

"Oh, but they are marrying into an old family that has been friends of their family for generations. It is truly a good marriage."

"So the father arranged all this," I said, beginning to catch on.

"Indeed. Our tribe does not leave the getting of a wife up to the young man. Our fathers say, 'You do not know these girls or their families. But we know their families. We know if they will make good wives. Just let us arrange it.' And so we do. Although some of the younger men are beginning to tell their fathers the girls that they would like to marry. Then their fathers will see if they can make an arrangement with that girl's father."

"I have read that you Somalis have a bride price. That a father may have to give ten, twenty, or even hundreds of camels for a girl. Is this true?"

"It's true if you are a bushman or if your father has camels!"

"But how about Abdulcadir's father?"

"He would have given money to pay the bride price."

"How much does a bride cost?"

"Do you want one?" Sherif's eyes shone with mischief.

"Of course I want a bride, but I cannot afford to buy one!" I retorted.

"You could get a wife for thirty shillings, or three hundred shillings, or three thousand shillings, depending on her family."

The musical trio had now returned to the platform to entertain the guests. We numbered about three or four hundred. Small boys ran through the crowd with trays of bottled Italian orange drink and glasses, Somali candy, and Italian cakes. Teenage fellows moved about shaking perfume on the guests from slim silver decanters which

136

looked like large salt and pepper shakers. Seated guests reached up with their hands to have them sprinkled, and tilted back their faces to have them brushed with drops of perfume. Over the white head of some particular elder or the tight wavy head of some favorite son, the perfume-shakers lingered a little longer.

"Ooh, it's lovely, but why?" I asked Sherif, after receiving my sprinkling.

"Oh, how can I say? It's just a custom. We do it to the guests because we honor them, and we do it because it is a happy time."

The evening air was laden with the rich, spicy odor of the perfume, an odor similar to the incense which they burned in their homes.

"Let's go back and wish Allah's blessings on the newly married men," Sherif suggested, rising from his chair to lead the way.

I followed, eager for the chance to talk with my student. We went behind the screen. Everyone seemed a little wild with the joy of the occasion. Old uncles and younger men were hugging the grooms, and laying their heads on their shoulders with their cheeks against their necks and mumbling blessings in Arabic. Smaller boys were tugging gleefully on the robes of their married relatives. Some old women were crooning.

"Sherif, what shall I do with this gift? I didn't know that five were being married. I brought a gift for only Abdulcadir. Now I am embarrassed to give it to him in front of the others."

"Oh, but it doesn't matter. Give it to me. I'll see that he gets it."

I had spent most of the morning in and out of first the Italian stores and then the Somali shops trying to find a gift. I had no idea whether the gift should favor the groom, or if I bought a gift to favor the bride, would it be a breach of etiquette? I finally decided on Italian chocolates in an elaborate box. I hoped that Abdulcadir would enjoy the chocolates and that his new young wife would find the fancy box a handy place to store pins, combs, and earrings.

I was not the only white person at the wedding. Several Italian men were there, too. But only one Italian, whom I discovered to be a professor of one of the grooms, and I went behind the screen to congratulate the fellows.

"Now stand with us, Mr. Eby, while we have our pictures taken." Abdulcadir was gently pulling me to his side. I had just congratulated all five of the grooms; Sherif was right at my side, introducing me to the elders, translating messages and inquiries for me and for his relatives.

So I stood with Abdulcadir, who was still dressed in his ceremonial clothes, to have our picture taken by a Somali photographer.

"And now, Mr. Eby, you shall go about the city with us in our wedding parade."

"But is it proper for a person like me to do this?" I asked, feeling a bit uncertain.

"Ha! Yes, and look! They are lining up to begin the walk. Come!"

I was pulled into position, with Abdulcadir on one side and Sherif on the other. We walked abreast with the other grooms.

In front of us were the singers and the drummer. Behind us a few old women were giving the joy cry and waving fans. The procession moved slowly, winding through the narrow street, cutting through an unpaved alley, across another street, through another alley, and then out on to another street, directly in front of the American Consulate building.

We were now on a main street, a block north of the square. The city's afternoon flow of traffic and pedestrians had begun to reach its peak. Our wedding parade shuffled along, half on the sidewalk, half on the street. Car horns blared at those bobbing along in the street; but no one seemed to take the drivers seriously. Shoppers stepped to doorways to avoid tangling with the paraders. Street-strollers, shambling along, having nothing of inter est to do, drifted in with the wedding-walkers and began singing and clapping their hands.

At first I was unaware of the stares I received from passers-by. Naturally they looked over the crowd to see who were the grooms, but when they saw my white face walking along abreast with the grooms, they stopped and stared. Some were caught completely off guard and laughed. Usually they asked someone on the edge of the wedding parade if I had taken a wife. Reassured that I had not taken a wife, but that I was the *ma'alim* of one of grooms, they continued on, relieved.

"Here, let Mr. Eby play one of the drums!"

Someone thrust a small hide drum into my hands.

"But I can't play!" I insisted. I was too embarrassed for such a public display of my ignorance.

Exactly at six-fifteen the procession halted before a mosque. The men all went inside and prayed. The old women shuffled off down an alley. I was left alone outside. They had windows in the mosque so I looked in and watched them kneeling and standing and going through their other religious gymnastics. Soon they were out.

"Now we will continue walking about, singing, and talking until nine o'clock."

"And then what?" I asked.

"Then we will deliver Abdulcadir and each of the other men to the houses to be left alone with their wives. The women are celebrating now back in the apartments. They will deliver the brides to the houses to meet their husbands." Sherif began to laugh. "Ho! Abdulcadir and his brothers have fears!"

"Well, who wouldn't?" I sympathized. "You yourself would have some fears to be left alone with a woman you never saw before."

"But they have been very clever." Sherif continued to chuckle.

"How?"

"We have a custom that the husband must remain alone in the house with his wife until the first Friday."

"So?"

"Well, this is Thursday. They can come out tomorrow and don't have to stay with their new wives! Many fellows do this when they don't know their wives. But if they do know them and love them, they'll get married on Saturday or Sunday and have a nice, long . . . ah . . . honeymoon! Is that what you call it?"

We laughed together. I then said that I was sorry but I had to leave the party and get back to the mission.

"Salaam, Mr. Eby."

"Salaam, Sherif," I echoed.

Chapter Thirteen

Half-Caste

The five o'clock English class was almost over. The hands of the clock showed ten minutes to six. At that time of the day in Somalia it was hard for me to concentrate on teaching. Evening was slipping in, flushing the glaring white-faced buildings of Mogadiscio with soft hues. The students were restless and inattentive, and I was beginning to drone incoherently.

I dismissed them early and they passed out of the room with "Good-bye, Mr. Teacher" or "I shall come Monday, Mr. Eby."

When I turned back to my desk, there stood Giuseppe, one of the many half-castes who lived somewhere down in the tight, stifling native section of the city.

"Teacher, can you help me?" he blurted out. "I want work."

I interrupted him with a wave to the nearest seat and then leaned against my desk.

"And what can you do? What work do you want?"

He made his fingers move rapidly over the top of the

141

desk as if he were typing and said, "What do you call this in English?" I told him the word and explained that neither I nor anyone here in the school would have enough work to keep a typist busy all day.

"Where did you learn this?" I asked.

"At the Catholic mission print shop."

"Don't they give you good money?"

"Nothing. I get a bed and some food for my work."

Well, I thought coolly, that's more than a lot of people in this city could say.

"But I didn't like living in the Catholic mission boarding school. . . . I have too many years age. I am seventeen," he argued. "I live now in a big house with other men . . . what do you call it . . . men with no wives? I want better work . . . and money to pay for living and eating there."

"But I have no need for a typist," I repeated.

For a moment I felt I could dismiss it at that. But there flashed before me the year when I was seventeen, the age of Giuseppe. I looked again at the boy as he sat before me. I smiled when I thought of Booth Tarkington and his book *Seventeen*. But I couldn't smile long, for it struck me that here was another seventeen-year-old, deliberately, yet unconsciously, trying to shake off the last of childhood and find his place among men. What he did not say and did not need to say, for that matter, was that he wanted some few coins of his own to jingle in his pockets, his first suit, or only a smartly cut pair of long dress trousers, or a tie perhaps. Whatever it was, did not matter. But something it must be! Something that he could wear and touch and secretly confide with himself that now surely he was a man.

"Where is your family? Where does your father work?"

He hesitated, searching my face. Slowly he smiled a

142

forced, crooked smile and said, "My father is English."

The statement jolted me. I straightened. "Where is he?" I asked. "What does he do? Have you ever seen him? Does he know that you are here?"

Slowly then, and with faltering eight-month-old English, and switching frequently to the Italian language, and using grotesque gestures, he told his story.

It was wartime in the early forties. North Africa and the Horn were just other places where the Allies clashed with the enemy. This time it was the pink British in their khaki shorts displaying pink, silly-grinning knees, and the black burly Bantu men. British and Bantu against Italian and Somali. It's all there in the history books—with detailed variations on the theme. The British took over the country then—the country previously known as Italian Somaliland. The city of Mogadiscio was full of Britishers. Most, of course, among them were the men of the military. And that's where Giuseppe's story really begins.

Giuseppe's Somali mother must have been frisky and custom-breaking in those earlier days, and the colonel probably went on a fling after the first break from duty. A few hours selfishly spent now created years of sorrow. But Giuseppe's mother is dead and her Somali tribe buried her with Muslim prayers.

"I have a paper here," Giuseppe said, producing it from his wallet. "It speaks about me and my father." This was a sudden change in our conversation. But then the whole thing had burst upon my placid classroom and orderly life all too suddenly.

"And are you a Somali citizen?" I asked, scanning the paper.

"No."

"Then an Italian citizen?"

"No, they said, 'Your father is not Italian.' "

"Well, what have the British done for you? Have they given you citizenship?" I asked.

"No. I speak to them often and show them this paper about me and my father, but they do nothing." He shrugged his shoulders.

Yes, I could imagine it all quite well. They do nothing. Well said, young man. But what could they do if the father did not want to have the child? Oh, they would be gracious, professionally kind about it, but totally unmoved. They would feel no attachment to his broken life. But what could I do, as an American in Somalia? Man without a country, I thought. But such a young man. Seventeen.

"Where does your father live?"

"My father live in Uganda; he live in a small village near Kampala," he responded.

When would they learn to put the "s" on the third person singular, I thought, sighing mentally. Then I was instantly angry. You're like a Pharisee, I snapped to myself, worrying about correctly crossing the "t" and dotting the "i"—worrying about the placing of an "s" while all the time a boy's life is torn in bitter conflict. Woe unto the Pharisees, I thought. Woe unto yourself, stupid!

"I wrote a letter to my father. I asked to come to live with him," Giuseppe added.

"You know his address? Did he reply? What did he tell you?" My questions tumbled out too rapidly and far too complicated for his comprehension. I repeated, "What did he tell you—in his letter?"

"My father has a white wife now and a daughter. He is old. He said I am not to come because he has a family and I cannot speak English. But I want to learn English,"

144

Giuseppe continued, "because he may say yes, for me to come if I speak English." There was a gleam of unabashed hope in his eyes as he finished speaking.

So this was the reason for his wanting to learn English, I thought.

"But it will take several years to learn to speak correctly," I suggested.

"But I like English; I will learn," he answered, with just the right tone of confidence in his voice.

He attended my class for several days. Then weeks passed, perhaps months, and I saw nothing of Giuseppe. He neither came to classes nor dropped by the house to chat as he had done a few times. He used to come hesitantly, almost fearfully at first. Later he was free and open. But always, when he did come, he would sit quietly, gazing out the window before speaking. And when he would turn to face me, his black eyes spoke dark and mysterious things.

One afternoon he came again. While I sat staring through the little apertures of the latticework, I saw him slip through the small iron gate and start up the path to my house.

He jabbed at the doorbell impatiently. Before I could get to the door from my desk, he rang it a second time. What's the rush, young man, I thought, as I swung the door open.

"Good evening, sir." He spoke with a ring in his voice.

"Good evening, Giuseppe. Come in. I haven't seen you for a long time. I thought maybe you went to Uganda."

As soon as I had said it, I hated myself for mentioning it so lightly. But he came to my rescue. "I am going to Uganda!" he cried, and could not keep from breaking into a small laugh. "My father wrote and said to come!"

"Sit down . . . here. Now tell me all—everything that happened these last weeks," I said, guiding him to a chair.

"Many weeks ago I wrote to my father again, and the British Consulate people wrote to him, too. The other day they told me to come to their office to see them. They showed me a letter from my father. It was a long letter with very difficult words. I could not understand much. But they told me that it said I was to go to him. *Meraviglioso!*" he exclaimed, ending in Italian.

It was the first time I had seen him laugh so freely—not with his old forced smile or steely laughter, but with the laugh of a person who had suddenly fallen in love with life.

"Mogadiscio is no good: no father, no mother, no brothers, no sisters . . . *niente.* . . ." he trailed off, the warm gleam dying in his eyes.

No, Mogadiscio was not kind to you, but would Uganda, 1,500 miles away, be better, I wondered. I could picture him, a golden brown half-caste, sipping tea at ten-twenty with his pink father, pink stepmother, and pink sister. But I couldn't think of it long—it seemed too hard.

"My father is not Catholic," ventured Giuseppe.

I nodded, knowingly, but I had not thought of that before.

"Yes, in my letter he said he wanted me to learn to be a Church of England person . . . what do you call it in English . . . *'protestante'?*"

"Protestant," I said wonderingly.

"I am Catholic. What must I do to be Protestant?" he asked, searching my face.

I felt helpless. I am a Christian, a firm Protestant, and a missionary, I thought. But how could I show him that theological concepts and church orders were not the things he needed to know now. That it was a person behind all

146

these matters whom he should know. And how could I explain all this, not knowing his language and he knowing only eight months of mine? I am not sure he even knew the word "pray"—at least not the word "sin."

"Do you have a Bible?" I stupidly asked.

"Bible—what is that?" he asked, looking at me blankly. "This," I said, picking up an English version. "I will give you an Italian Testament."

"Thank you," he said, impressed.

I suddenly remembered the season and the dirt roads. "We are in the rainy season, you know. The roads to Kenya and Uganda will be closed for at least a month or more yet until they are dry enough for cars or lorries to pass."

"*Si! Si!* But it will take many days until I get a passport and a visa. I want to buy some clothes and finish my job. Three weeks, four weeks, or five weeks—it does not matter. The good thing is that I am going!"

Days passed into weeks. I followed the ins and outs of my routine teaching in the mission school. And in the passing of days, Giuseppe and his troubled life passed from my immediate consciousness.

But one afternoon in August, Giuseppe returned. I had been so absorbed in painting the rusty iron gate that I did not hear anyone coming.

"Mr. Eby." The voice startled me.

"Oh, Giuseppe. . . ." But I left the greeting unfinished when I saw the tightness in his face.

"I received a telegram from Uganda," he said abruptly. "I do not go." From the pocket of his faded blue shirt he pulled the crumpled telegram and held it up for me to read.

"FATHER DIES HEART ATTACK STOP RE-QUESTED REMAIN MOGADISCIO STOP LETTER

FOLLOWS." That was all it said. Just a few neatly blocked letters readable at a glance. And in the few seconds that he held it up I was able to reread it. There was no use turning it over carefully, hoping to find more words—nicer words. There wouldn't be any. It was here, a few words—cold, terse, decisive.

I looked at him and he held my eyes with his for a burning, searching second. They were black and spoke dark, mysterious things. And then it was gone—the light had gone out in his eyes. They narrowed and were dull.

He turned then to leave. And for one short moment I caught the tightening of the muscles in his face, the firm set of his jaw, the straight line of his lips. The young love and laughter had drained from him. He had found his place among men. But such a young man among such men. Men who would never laugh freely or love openly. Men for whom life was a series of bitter surprises. Yes, he had found his place among men. But such a young man. Seventeen.

Chapter Fourteen

Ali/Jama

Dear Eby:

I left Mogadiscio on January 19, 1960—a day when I left almost everything with it. But I have not stopped remembering you. How can I forget you. There is no reason at all. First, you are my real teacher in English, and second, a friend who was always ready to help me in any difficult circumstance. Then how can I forget you? Believe me, that I am neither joking nor flattering, but speaking to you frankly and truly.

When I was in the plane and looking out through the small windows (I don't know how to describe such a circumstance), I did not see a single person, except you standing there, waving your both hands to us. If I interpreted correctly, it was doubtlessly a sign of affection and of good hope.

I am happy that my brother is continuing to learn English from you and becoming a friend of yours. It is a great pleasure to see a brother occupy a place where before him was his older brother.

Really, I am very tired and cannot continue writing to you. It is Ramadan, and I am fasting. My stomach is burning like a hell, my mind does not work properly, and my eyes make clouds.

Your kind letter arrived. I wish you could see how proud and happy I was at the very instant I received it. But at the same time I was ashamed. It was not for you to write to us first, but on the contrary. It was our duty to write you as soon as we arrived here. I beg your pardon for having delayed in writing to you.

I must stop now. I wish you good life till your departure.

That was the gist of two letters I received a month after two of my best English students had accepted scholarships to complete their secondary training in Kenya.

It was a humbling thing to receive such warm letters from students. Surely every teacher has experienced the joy of having one turn back to thank him for his efforts. Yet it was different with Ali and Jama. In the last months before their leaving, our teacher-student relationship had evolved into an almost brother-brother relationship.

Of my nearly one hundred students, no others were able to successfully bridge that awesome gulf between student and teacher. Some tried, but their attempts were irritating or awkward.

Within the limitations of my profession as a teacher, and the reverence an African has for that position, I extended to my students as casual a situation as I could create without completely destroying their image of my profession. Only Ali and Jama reached out and fully comprehended that offer. Only they of my students moved about me, never colliding, never cringing. Only they looked me levelly in the eye, never up to me, never down on me.

A few weeks before the two fellows left for Kenya, I

invited them to the house to eat dinner with us. I had a few small fears about the success of the evening. Ali and Jama, I knew, came from very nice homes. But they had both told me, when accepting the invitation, that they had never eaten a meal in the home of a European. It was a new adventure for them. I had no fear of their being able to cope with European manners; I was only concerned about creating as relaxed and informal an atmosphere as possible.

A meal shared together is a gesture of friendliness. Social differences and varying interests are often dissolved around so common an object as food. People are always inviting or being invited to dinners. A businessman will eat with a prospective client, or a fellow with his girl, each hoping by this informal occasion to influence the other. And so it was with our evening. The act of sharing a meal together helped to dissolve certain barriers.

Strangely enough, it was they who turned the conversation to the topic of religions. One of the amazing discoveries these fellows made was the wide difference in practice between my religion and the Catholic religion of the Italians. Almost paradoxically the similarity between Christianity and their Islamic religion was equally an amazement for them. Such were the things we talked about for many hours.

"What do you really believe will happen to me as a Muslim when I die?"

"Ali, my friend, I am not a judge!"

"No, but, what does your religion teach about people who are not Christians when they die?"

"We Christians are never to judge; we are only to forgive."

"But what does your Bible say about people who do not believe in Jesus as the Son of God?"

"One little verse says, 'There is none other name under heaven given among men, whereby we must be saved.' "

"That's in the Bible?"

"Yes, and one time Jesus said, 'If ye believe not that I am he, ye shall die in your sins.' "

"Those are strong words."

"Yes."

"What else does it say?"

"Jesus said some very comforting words. 'I am come that they might have life, and that they might have it more abundantly.' "

"Muhammad said some very wonderful words, too!"

"I know—and some very poetic ones. I read the Koran."

"You did? How?"

"In English. It has been translated."

"Did you like it?"

"Some. But some parts were duller than parts of our Bible!"

"Even I will agree."

My plans for returning to the States included a layover in Nairobi, Kenya. The layover would be two days after school closed for Ali and Jama in Mombasa. We began planning for a rendezvous at the Nairobi YMCA. A year had passed since I had seen them, and I was eager for this last contact. Two days and two nights we could be together.

Then suddenly the Aden Airways reshuffled its schedules. Its weekly flight to Nairobi would drop me there two days before school closed for Ali and Jama. They could not possibly make it to Nairobi in time, and I could not possibly lay over four days. Their replies to this change of plans were interesting. Wrote Jama, "I almost came to curse the staff of Aden Airways Company, who changed their flight just in a moment which we were about to meet each other, converse, and walk together along the nice streets of Nairobi.

"If that is the case, I think it is something already ordained by the Omnipotent, the Creator of all whom we are bound, only to bear whatsoever happens to us.

"Since the day in which we have received your first letter, up to now, we were looking forward to your previously fixed day, to meet each other in Nairobi. We were looking to it, believe me, like when we seek the sight of the moon in the month of Ramadan."

Wrote Ali, "Your most appreciated letter arrived to me while I was at dinner. I was so eager to see it contents that I could not help wanting to see it before I was finished eating.

"But such rapture did not last long for me. Here I am suddenly struck by the grievous news that our so-longed-for meeting in Nairobi is not going to take place. I am most sorry about it. If you could imagine how I was looking forward to meeting you in Nairobi.

"Mr. Omar, you were our dearest friend and our teacher. It is very bitter to know that there is not any other alternative which would have made our meeting possible so that we could see you once again. But what can we do? Let the laws of nature take its course.

"I wish you a good journey, a prosperous life in your future; a life full of happiness, enjoyment, and devotion to the Creator. May God conserve your health. Doubtless one day you will marry and for that occasion I pray that you produce six sons and one daughter. Will that do?"

This was not the first that my offspring had been discussed by Ali and Jama. One Saturday, the school being closed, Ali, Jama, and I spent the morning at the beach.

153

The beach was generally quite empty in the mornings, except Sunday, when the Italians swarmed over it, having gotten Mass out of the way.

It was a typical blue-white-hot day. But the breeze from the ocean eased the morning glare. We swam some, and they were very good at it. But mostly we lay talking on the white sand.

"So you are soon leaving me, going away to become greatly educated," I said, teasingly.

"Oh, but Mr. Eby, you know that we are only going to Kenya to finish our secondary education."

"We are going there so we will be forced to use English constantly," put in Jama.

"A good idea," I said.

"This should help us to get a scholarship for some university in America, when we come back and our English is very good."

"I hope that you will win a scholarship to an American college. Then I can be a friend to you there as you have been to me here."

"If not America, then Britain," offered Jama.

"Or even Italy."

"For what do you want to study?" I asked.

"I want to be a medical doctor." Ali was the first to respond.

"And I," Jama began hesitantly, "sometimes I want to be a doctor, but usually I want to be a veterinarian. I will probably be that."

"It all sounds very nice."

"So, Mr. Eby, after you have gone to America to visit your family and friends and have got a wife and returned again to teach in Mogadiscio, I will be here to deliver your wife's babies!" Ali chuckled.

"And I will deliver your cow's calf," said Jama dryly.

We rolled over in the sand, laughing.

"And I shall live to be very old and teach all your children. And I shall beat them if they do not learn their English as well as you have!"

Ali's home was the first and only student's home I ever had occasion to visit during my three years of teaching in Mogadiscio. At first it bothered me considerably, that I was not invited into the homes of my students. Any missionary woman teacher of the girls' or women's classes was constantly being invited out. I thought that our missionary standard of living was so high above that of my students that they would be embarrassed to invite me to their homes. I also thought that perhaps I had not established a very good rapport with my students, even after a year. However, I was to discover that all those thoughts were misinterpretations.

The social pattern of Mogadiscio was not that of the bush villages. Guests were seldom entertained in homes, unless you were a government official with a small mansion. On the ordinary level of teacher-student relationships, it simply was not done. Rather, I was always being invited for tea with a student or students to some teashop down town, or even sometimes to a Somali restaurant. There in the cool evening, under municipal lighting, at a sidewalk café, the student would entertain his teacher.

However, students gladly accepted my invitations to come into my house for tea, a meal, or just to sit in the shade on the veranda and talk.

Ali lived just off a noisy street of shops with an uncle, a kind, intelligent old man. Our frequent night strolls through the city after the school closed would occasionally bring us to sit on the stoop of his uncle's house and to talk, sometimes with his uncle and other relatives. On one occasion, Ali invited me in to see his room, but not without dashing in first to straighten it up a bit, as any of us might have done.

I was home in the States for over a year when one day a strange envelope was slid into my mailbox. It bore a Russian postage stamp. In the corner of the envelope, the return address carried Ali's name, and a Moscow address.

Stunned, I put the letter into my pocket and carried it about with me for some time. However, when I caught myself pretending that I had not received any letter, I pulled it from my pocket and made myself open it.

The warm greetings, the apologies for not writing, and then, "You will probably wonder how I happen to be in Moscow! It's very easy to explain. When I came back to Mogadiscio, from Kenya, the Somali government had awarded me another scholarship, this time to the U.S.S.R. to study medicine with twenty other Somali students who had completed their secondary school education. I am very happy here in Moscow and my studies are getting along fine. . . ."

I remembered our last evening together. I had taken them in the mission car twenty miles to the little village of Afgoi, a lovely setting on the banks of the Shebeli. There we ate a supper together, walked, and talked, took pictures of each other, and pledged ourselves to write to each other in the years to come.

Eventually, I had strength enough to take up a pen and write to Ali in Moscow. At first I was bitter that he was there, bitter at the stupid American government representatives in Mogadiscio that would miss some of these most brilliant fellows in the slow grind of their red tape, bitter that he had not the sense to refuse to study in a communist country, bitter at the idea that I may truly never see him again, or if I did, he would be a stranger. But God gave me strength to confess my bitterness and to write and wish Ali success and a blessing.

Again he wrote. "I don't know why you don't write to me. I had sent a letter to you from Moscow in which I had explained all the circumstances which had hindered me from writing to you earlier. I had hoped that you would forgive me of my negligence, but your long silence makes me think that you have decided to do otherwise. I am sure that evening in which we had a nice time in Afgoi and on the way back to Mogadiscio I had promised you that I would write you as long as I live. This promise I really intend to fulfill, and that is why I insist in writing you despite your perpetual silence. Believe me, it is grievous not to hear from you. . . ."*

Why didn't my letters get through to him? Were they being lost? Or tampered with? Would that God could somehow watch over my letters to Ali, to let him know that I think of him, that I write to him, that I pray for him.

And Jama? His letters have been even less. Yet I feel within me that he has not forgotten our friendship. At the airport, when they were leaving to take up their scholarships, it was Jama who embraced me, pulling my head on his shoulder against his neck while he laid his head against my neck and shoulder.

And then I remember Ali's kind old uncle saying, "Eby is ours and we are his." And again I am broken and humbled.

*Since this chapter was written, the author has had exchanges of letters with Ali and Jama.

157

Epilogue

All day some snatches of a Negro spiritual had been singing their way through my head. "Goin' home, goin' home;
I'm just goin' home. . . ." But part of this moving song
(if I remembered correctly) was not quite true in my case.
"Work's all done; care's laid by. . . ." Even though the
examinations were corrected and the certificates issued
and the summary typed and now lying somewhere on
Brother Director's desk, I still hadn't been able to acquire
that satisfied feeling of having the work all sewed up. My
work in the mission didn't seem to end. But I suppose
that no one's work ever really ends, regardless of what he
has been trying to do. We just have to lay our tools down
in the sun and go take a little rest in the shade.

I startled the other occupants of the house (too frequently I fear) by giving voice to something near to a
dramatic rendition to the chorus of the "Goin' Home
Song" that kept reaching shouting crescendos in my head.
But it was legitimately lodged—the song I mean—because
it was ten o'clock at night and that meant it was only

eighteen hours until I board the first plane for the first leg of my journey home. But it was the short leg of my speedy five-legged home-going monster. And it ran something like this: Mogadiscio, Nairobi, Addis Ababa, Cairo, Athens, Frankfurt, London, New York.

I remembered the night I announced to my students that this would be the last month of my teaching them. It seemed so far away then, but suddenly it was there. So, with a paradoxical eager-reluctance I handed over my classes to other folks round the mission.

After the students had all noisily filed through the door that last night, I slowly erased the blackboard and snapped out the light. Stepping into the adjacent room which served as the chapel, I sat down and rested my head on the back of a chair.

In those few moments the past three years rose before me—vaguely and deliberate at first, like a shallow, silver stream from some sphere, but rising to a full and deep tide with wave after wave of memories crashing in on the shore of my senses. And in those few moments a strong condemning sense of failure filled me.

What had I really done for Jesus among the few Muslim students who regularly attended my English classes? Whom had I "led to Christ"? And now I was leaving them to go to my Christian homeland. So I prayed to God that some other young fellow or couple would become acquainted with this work and would in a few months come to live and learn with my Somali Muslim students.

With the ending of my teaching, the inevitable lining up for picture-taking followed. Photography was still such a new thing to Somalia that nothing but the most formal poses were considered acceptable for picture-taking. Casual, informal poses were sacrilegious to the very goddess of photography! So we stood like so many shiny, tin soldiers, with never a flash of a smile.

My scheduled going away called for farewell parties. Thus one night we played a few games, served up some local highly spiced tea and orange drink with *zamboozies* (a triangular pastry shell chucked full of ground meat, onions, and red peppers). Such an occasion also demanded the letter of appreciation (there was always one of these) previously prepared by the students and then read some time near the end of the party. The letter was flooded with flowery phrases of praise, high-sounding, inappropriate words of honor, and usually some badly mangled English. But it was all well meant. And that time I nearly believed much of it.

It was not the time to be leaving Somalia! Not when nature was at her best. But then to stand and watch the blue-green ocean come pounding in and breaking white on the beach, to see the glimmer of the country plains, fresh from the rains—that was not the place to receive "a call of God" to work in Somalia.

One must go down to the tight, dark sections of town, and there in the thronging, dusty streets, with frequent bitter odors, see and feel the throb of the people; or sit for hours with some student, who with drained face, tells you why he can't believe Jesus is the Son of God. There was the place to receive "a call."